# THE UNTAMED GOD

*Unleashing the Supernatural in the Body of Christ*

Neil B. Wiseman

Beacon Hill Press of Kansas City
Kansas City, Missouri

ISBN 083-411-6294

Printed in the United States of America

Cover Design: Paul Franitza

**Library of Congress Cataloging-in-Publication Data**
Wiseman, Neil B.
    The untamed God : unleashing the supernatural in the body of Christ /
Neil B. Wiseman.
      p.  cm.
    Includes bibliographical references.
    ISBN 0-8341-1629-4 (hardback)
    1. Miracles—Case studies.  2. Supernatural.  I. Title.
BT97.2.W57    1997
231.7—dc21
                                      96-46719
                                        CIP

10  9  8  7  6  5  4  3  2  1

# DEDICATED TO MORE THAN 1,200 STUDENTS

Your do-or-die devotion to Christ
keeps teaching me amazing lessons
about how the Supernatural enriches life
and empowers service.
Don't be surprised if you find your tracks
throughout this book.

\* \* \*

# APPRECIATION AND THANKS

Writing a book feels a lot like mountain climbing. Sometimes the views are spectacular. Sometimes the climb feels like sheer drudgery. Energy, oxygen, and food are absolutely essential for the journey. Always, companions on the way make the ascent more enjoyable. I had help for this journey from many friends. Special thanks to the Beacon Hill publishing team, to my Nazarene Bible College colleagues, and to Bonnie—my wife, partner, and best friend.

# WHO SHOULD READ THIS BOOK?

All who pray for the renewal of the Church and the redemption of humankind are urged to read this book:

### Lay leaders
serious about building miraculous, life-changing churches.

### Pastors
longing for spiritual reality in their congregations.

### Denominational leaders
willing to pay any price to make the church
vibrant during their watch.

### Sunday School teachers
yearning to make an eternal impact on their pupils.

### College and university professors
desiring to develop students to transform the world.

### Committed teens
wanting to make their lives count in our kind of world.

### Parachurch CEOs and personnel
hungering for their ministries to impact the globe.

### Every believer
eager to see Christ transform our world.

# CONTENTS

# FOREWORD

## WE NEED THE SUPERNATURAL

*The Untamed God* could revolutionize your ideas about the Church of Jesus Christ. Read it expecting to be impacted and assured.

The miraculous "something more" of the gospel is missing in far too many contemporary churches. Too often we pray, serve, and promote in our own strength and cleverness and then wonder why we achieve mere human results. It's time for believers to rediscover the supernatural power of God.

*The Untamed God* sounds a serious summons to encourage us to use supernatural muscle in the service of Christ. Here's a call to recognize the significance of personal purity on the outcomes of ministry. Here's a challenge to seek supernatural guidance for every leadership responsibility. Here's a reminder that we must have God's anointing on our preaching and that we can be strengthened by cultivating the divine-nearness in our praying. Here's an invitation to recover the presence of Christ in our caring for others. Here's a challenge to see how God uses fully yielded ecclesiastic authority for Kingdom achievements.

It's time that Christians allow God to work miracles in every church and every individual expression of ministry. Sadly, too many contemporary churches have lost their grip on the force that makes them a unique power in the world today—the supernatural, transforming, life-changing power of Christ. That's a serious flaw. For without holy empowerment, all our competence, preparation, programming, facilities, and sacrifices produce dissatisfying results.

*The Untamed God* implores us to take Christianity's new-life-for-old enablement to the cutting edge of the spiritual wastelands around us. While coaxing the church to leave her comfort zone, Neil Wiseman underscores the fact that divine empowerment usually comes in full measure to those who set out to do world-changing exploits for God. It's time to seize the unparalleled challenges and opportunities all around us.

Let us discover for ourselves what the Early Church leaders knew well and what the founding parents of every religious movement have experienced firsthand. All contemporary Christian leaders—ministers and laypersons—can access the power of an untamed God.

Dr. John C. Maxwell
Founder and President, INJOY Ministries

# PREFACE

## THE SUPERNATURAL—A HOLY VITALITY FOR CHRISTIAN LEADERS

For years I have mused about the availability of supernatural resources for parish ministry. Various experiences, discussions, and readings have shaped my thinking about miraculous factors in such a ministry. But the most compelling reason for writing this book is the incredible need for the supernatural in the contemporary Church. The pressing question before us is this: How can we identify and cultivate the mysterious, wonderful place in which our finest work and divine aid meet? I also welcome an opportunity to celebrate the supernatural empowerment I have so often enjoyed in my service to Christ.

Attempting to connect holy enablement and human effort, this book builds on the following foundational principles.

• **The supernatural is not always sensational.** I heard a powerful preacher declare, "The supernatural need not be spectacular. It might be common and ordinary, like a baby's birth, a sunset, a beggar helping another find bread, or God's transformation of a human being." Church leaders sometimes settle for spiritual iciness because they fear wildfire.

• **The supernatural cannot be thoroughly explained.** A clergy educator remarked with tongue in cheek, "We must exercise extreme caution about anything we can't explain logically—as if anyone could explain the Incarnation, redemption, the Resurrection, or what Paul called the 'mysteries of grace.'" Though we cannot fully explain love or compassion or caring or commitment, we know they are real.

Likewise, the supernatural is not invalidated just because finite minds cannot fully comprehend it.

• **The supernatural is a joyous resource to experience.** A former and much loved student of mine called to talk about his first Sunday in his first pastorate. He reported with joy, "I preached the best I could, but something happened as I preached that I can't explain. I said more than I was capable of saying. I said exactly what needed to be said with insight, tenderness, and tough love. How do you explain this happening to a beginner like me? Is this a holy anointing?" It seems my friend was on the right track.

• **The supernatural need not frighten us.** When I first discussed the ideas for this book with a religious book editor friend, he immediately expressed uneasiness about words like "supernatural" and "miraculous." He wisely cautioned that writers and publishers must be careful not to wound the Church by labeling strange, eccentric, or even peculiar notions as "supernatural" and "miraculous." Some mistakenly believe that any weird action or position taken by a strange friend of Jesus is supernatural.

Of course, there are some outrageous or excessive practices in the Church. But because some mistaken follower of Christ journeys to the outer edge is no reason to ignore or even scorn a balanced and biblical view of what God wants to do through people like us in our time, in our setting.

• **The supernatural is greatly needed now.** Perhaps the most pressing issue of contemporary Christianity is how desperately today's Church needs a supernatural intervention. Consider the spiritual sterility and devotional dryness all around us. Congregations hunger for an anointed word from God. Preachers are frustratingly trying to win and nurture broken people with human rationality or scholarly insights from the social sciences. Believers wonder if God works through their commitments of energy, devotion, time, and generosity. Secularists, bored by meaninglessness, might be drawn to Christ if they were convinced the Church offered supernatural transformations and authentic fulfillment.

Think how desperate our world is. We are confused by

12

institutions that have let us down, like hospitals, schools, post offices, and welfare programs. We are bankrupted of values. We are disappointed by civic leaders. We are frightened by how crippled our churches have become. And we feel disillusioned by the mistaken promises of science. We need God.

• **The supernatural is biblical.** This moment in human history cries out for miraculous empowerment like what the Church possessed in Bible times. Our families, friends, communities, churches, and world are starving for a miraculous intervention of God. Let's recover the supernatural factors that shout from nearly every page of Scripture.

We need God to do through us what we can never do on our own. It's time to shut down the activity whirlwind so we can feed our souls. It's time to seek the Source so that our preaching, pastoral care, decision making, and implementation of mission will pulsate with miraculous effectiveness. When we recover this supernatural force, we will be plugged into a vigorous force for righteousness and achievement.

God never intended that ministry would be done with human strength or finite wisdom. He had something incredibly stronger and loftier in mind when He promised empowerment from beyond so that we can do and be more than we thought possible.

We need not attempt ministry alone when we can be linked with Omnipotence.

# 1

# The Supernatural— Unique Resources for Renewal

## *Contagious Christlikeness for Secular Society*

Paul Harvey recently reported on his radio show, "According to a study I just reviewed of people between the ages of 21 and 40, over 40 percent answered 'Yes' when asked the question 'Do you believe in UFOs?'"[1] Accounts from assorted sources demonstrate a rising interest in the unknown that goes well beyond unidentified flying objects (UFOs) to what the apostle Paul called "the powers of this dark world and . . . spiritual forces of evil in the heavenly realms" (Eph. 6:12).

Evidence of this fascination is striking and growing. Increasingly, newspapers, magazines, and television commentators focus on the mystical and mysterious and on crystals and meditation. Books about angels, pop spirituality, and out-of-body experiences top best-seller lists. Thousands of secularists, weary of meaninglessness, keep initiating questions about the inner life and the world beyond. Queries about the supernatural and miraculous are being asked continually outside and inside the Church. Concerning the current craze in which angels appear on magazine covers, women's dresses, wallpaper, men's ties, and note cards, an old saint observed, "The supporting cast gets more attention than the main Figure—the Christ."

In spite of this climate of spiritual search in surprising places, much of the church world is silent about the supernatural, miraculous, and transcendent. Any force, experience, or presence that cannot be seen, touched, or defined is downplayed or ignored. As a result, creation, the Incarnation, miracles, and the Resurrection—all awesome wonders of biblical faith—are lost to a new generation and no longer create justifiable awe in the people of God. But to this muddled mix of concepts, an additional factor voiced by a third world missionary must be added. He said, "If we do not emphasize the supernatural where I live and serve, the people refuse to listen and then go back to the witch doctor, who they think has supernatural qualities."

There is no question that a growing fascination about the supernatural and the miraculous is all around us. Can the Church ignore the hunger and thirst behind this curiosity without being guilty of malfeasance of duty? Can she downplay it without, in fact, abandoning a significant part of her mission? Are we willing to lose so much of what God intended His Church to be? No! We need the supernatural and the miraculous. Our times need more than human achievement and worthy rational efforts. We need much more of God to help us think more than we have yet thought and to help us accomplish more than we have ever been able to do.

## CONSIDER MY BAD DREAM

After pondering this disparity between interest in the supernatural in the culture and the scarcity of the supernatural in the Church, I had a dream the other night. Maybe it was a nightmare. But in it every vestige of the supernatural set sail for some faraway destination that I can't remember. I thought we might breathe more easily after the departure, because the contemporary Church would be freed from explaining the unexplainable.

I stood in my dream at the Statue of Liberty, watching the ship *Supernatural* grow dim in the distance. At first I felt good about the parting. As the boat grew smaller and smaller on the horizon, I thought, "The Church's problems will ease now. No more mysteries. No more outbursts about life-transforming faith. No more debates about the difference between the spiritual and the secular. No more uncomplicated saints who see things too simply. And no more questions I can't answer."

Think of the changes I observed at church. No more prayer meetings with mature believers—secularism and rationalism do not have much need for intercession and fasting. No more prayer and fasting for missions. No more believing God for the return of the prodigal or believing for an attitude change for the stay-at-home son. No more petitions for healings. No more commitments from rosy-cheeked youth who believe God called them to take the gospel to the world. No more sacrificial giving for Kingdom causes. No more Christ-inspired hospitals for healing the sick or for searching for cures for cancer, heart disease, or sickle-cell anemia. No more believing beyond seeing.

And in my dream the Church stopped preaching on supernatural biblical themes like the Incarnation, Resurrection, or Second Coming—all of that is too supernatural for the new climate of the Church. Then, too, since miracles had become off-limits, we could not discuss the feeding of the 5,000, the healing of a leper, the turning of the water into wine at a wedding, the healing of a soldier's severed ear, or Paul's conversion on the Damascus road.

The saddest part of the dream was how shallow the Church seemed. Without prayer, sacrifice, fasting, and much of the Bible, our church service seemed much like Rotary Club or school board meetings or the weekly meeting of the social workers down at the social services department of our county.

In my sleep I tried hard to catch one last glimpse of the good ship *Supernatural*. It was to be my last sight of the Church as the hands and feet and mind of Christ in the world.

Then I awoke in a cold sweat. How glad I am that my dream was not real—at least not yet!

## IS THE MAIN THING THE MAIN THING NOW?

"Almost nothing is happening," complained an astute student in one of my classes.

Though I thought he might be referring to a meeting of the student council, late Saturday afternoon on Main Street in small-town America, or our college library during Monday night football, he was in fact deploring the loss of spiritual vitality in liberal as well as conservative churches across North America.

I started to argue, citing the laudable activities that make many churches virtual beehives of activity. I reminded him of strong struggles sponsored by the Church dealing with militarism and racism and abortion. I reminded him of attempts to reform sexist language in hymns and prayers. I reminded him about Meals on Wheels for shut-ins and political action committees to encourage voters to make intelligent choices at the polls.

And before he could reply, I thought to add to the argument a reminder about solemn assemblies where the economic, political, and social issues are hashed and rehashed. I thought I could tell him about bureaucracies that lead whole families of churches toward so-called worship reforms and endless ecclesiastical reorganizations. And what about fellowship meals and church bowling teams?

What my friend meant, as he explained later, is that the contemporary Church is so busy doing many laudable things that it neglects its main mission—gospel impact on unbelievers and the spiritual care of Christians. We are shackled by superficiality.

In many church discussion forums the supernatural is debated and criticized. The more pressing issue, however, is that the supernatural is not always considered a vital ingredient of the Church. But without it the Church is a sad, ineffective miniature of General Motors or the United States Army. Without it our buildings are shrines to what we could be. Without it our planning goes nowhere. Without it our personnel are undermotivated and easily discouraged. Without it our preaching is mere human opinion and do-goodism. Without the supernatural the Church is an anemic replica of the world and its systems.

The Church today experiences all kinds of confusion and difficulty because the main thing is not the main thing. So the Church is like the restaurant beside the freeway that started selling gasoline to attract more people to the restaurant. Without meaning to do so, the new oil products dealer soon sold more gas than food. Though his business by the freeway is an economic success, it's no longer much of a restaurant despite what the sign out front says.

This Neil Wiseman homemade restaurant parable reminds us of the contemporary Church. Perhaps without intending to do so, the Church in many places has largely deserted its distinctive and supernatural sphere of operation. Much of the Church's praiseworthy efforts could be achieved as well by civic clubs, public schools, community agencies, and charitable trusts. But none of these other agencies even consider doing what Jesus created the Church to do, nor would we want them to try.

As a result, the Church's reason for being is neglected, and her mission remains unfulfilled in contemporary society. The salt is not salty, and the light flickers under a bushel. The Church, having abandoned her distinctive reason for being, no longer needs God's empowering energy. This may be the reason we have such a debilitating malaise in contemporary life.

My student friend's reasoning is right. Working on secondary causes is magnificent, provided the Church does not give up on what it alone can do. From a secularist's viewpoint, we must ask why anyone should go to church to receive what can better be found somewhere else.

## THE SUPERNATURAL: DEFINITIONS AND DESCRIPTIONS

The supernatural was God's idea. Examples of divine intervention in common events are recorded on nearly every page of Scripture. But we are confused. For some in our time, the supernatural represents a complex, emotionally charged spiritual high, while for others it simply means an inspired common awareness of the nearby-ness of God. Essentially, the supernatural is the difference between what the church so often is and what it could be.

• **The supernatural provides a "surprising plus."** In day-by-day operational terms in any church, the supernatural means enablement from God to convince thought, challenge wills, win affections, nurture emotions, and cherish fellowship relations so as to develop an ongoing maturity in Christ. "Supernatural" describes any Kingdom event that goes beyond human ability—it is the "surprising plus" God adds to our best efforts.

• **The supernatural provides connectedness.** The word "supernatural" implies the possibility that Christian workers can connect with God as the Source of all Kingdom efforts. The supernatural allows us to learn—sometimes it may be slow and halting—that satisfying Christian service at its best is a shared experience at an intersection where human need, Christian action, and God meet.

Sadly, the miraculous elements of Kingdom interests have been squeezed out of ministry so leaders are often viewed, or sometimes view themselves, as directors of beneficial social activities, overseers of ventures to curb human suffering, protectors of the institutional church, or pop psychologists who resolve emotional problems for the people from the pulpit—or all of the above. Then spiritual issues are played down, trivialized, or bypassed altogether.

• **The supernatural is not always spectacular.** Columnist Peggy Noonan started me thinking about nonspectacular miracles in life: "I believe in miracles. The way I see it, life isn't flat and thin and 'realistic'; it's rich and full of mystery and surprise. I think miracles exist in part as gifts and in part as clues that there is something beyond the flat world we see. I also think they happen every day, from the baby's perfect shoulder in the sonogram to saints performing wonders."[2]

Try taking those ideas into the work of your church. Clearly, God's involvement in human affairs can be supernatural without being spectacular or sensational. The miraculous does not depend on large numbers, proper feelings, loud prayers, or even impressive spiritual maturity; but it does require complete dependence on God. A lot of truly supernatural ministry is accomplished in such a natural or predictable way that a leader or congregation may not be aware of the transcendence of God in their circumstances.

Think of all the nonspectacular ways "the Holy Other" saves souls, heals dysfunctional families, directs changing seasons in nature, and shields us from calamity. Something that appears quite ordinary may be miraculous. The grace of God that opens a child's mind like a spring flower to the ways of faith is as much a miracle as a skid row alcoholic finding religion in a rescue mission. The influence of a Christian character that succeeds in pointing a seeking youth to the Savior is every bit as supernatural as the physician who saves his patient from death. Or consider the quiet ways God adds a supernatural dimension to our preaching, worship, pastoral care, and administrative efforts.

Then, too, I love to think of the so-called natural miracle the Father orchestrates in the safe arrival of a newborn, an event about which Darrell Jodock of Muhlenberg College so tenderly comments: "A person can understand every detail of anatomy, genetics, fetal development, and obstetrics and still be amazed by the mystery of childbirth. Added information often enhances the sense of mystery one feels holding a living, breathing baby who previously did not exist. This kind of mystery has inexhaustible depth. It is complex. It intensifies joy and sadness. It beckons and frightens, and is unlike anything to which we are accustomed."[3]

All this means, of course, that the supernatural sometimes appears routine and predictable simply because we have experienced God supernaturally so often in simple, predictable events of our days; human life and conversion, to name two, are common but supernatural. The message of this book pleads for a rediscovery of the nonspectacular, nonsensational, but supernatural dimensions of Christian service in sensible, reenergizing ways.

● **The supernatural makes ministry effective.** "Supernatural," as I am using the word, can be defined as allowing divine enablement to so completely saturate all phases of ministry that the people we serve will be molded into Christ-likeness, that we are personally challenged to invest our best efforts in the Kingdom, and that the Church will be restored to being a distinctive righteous force in contemporary character and culture.

"Supernatural" describes a process in a congregation in which people are magnetically drawn to a worshiping fellowship—a place where the person, message, and ministry of Jesus are the wellspring of all that is done.

● The supernatural helps us recognize "the Mysterious Other." "Supernatural" describes how God works in the Body of Christ through tough circumstances, extraordinary breakthroughs, and astounding advancements that would not be possible in human strength, ingenuity, perseverance, or piety.

Supernatural—a full recognition and welcome of "the Mysterious Other"—means allowing ministry to be filled to the brim with divine enablement and eternal significance. Then the Church becomes appealing and invincible because it is unique and is so needed in the lives of people who have previously experienced only bland, trite religion. Then superficial religion gets transformed into supernatural impact. Then service is done as an act of worship and obedience to a God who is lofty, majestic, loving, and who deserves from us a response of wonder and adoration.

## HAVE WE GIVEN UP TOO MUCH?

Have we given up too much by trying to add excitement and interest while abandoning our mission?

Have we given up too much when we allow people to remain morally where they are rather than preaching and practicing the possibilities of a supernatural transformation of human character?

Have we given up too much when evil forces like the alcohol industry, drug dealers, crooked civic officials, and biased media no longer fear the righteousness of God as communicated through the Church?

Have we given up too much when people inside and

outside the Church no longer expect the Church to be a force for righteousness in our world?

Have we given up too much when whole segments of society are interested in a religiously oriented social institution that has no more life-changing impact on people than government programs offered elsewhere in our towns and cities?

Have we given up too much in abandoning the supernatural in the affairs of the nation? How bad does government have to get before the redeemed of God begin to change it? How many mediocre or crooked politicians do we have to endure before we turn our nations to God?

For some hard-to-understand reason, many contemporary churches and their leaders have embraced a stubborn and disastrous affinity to make preaching, pastoral care, worship, and Christian service lethargic, monotonous, and deficient of the supernatural. Sadly, such lifeless religion long ago lost its appeal, so the masses no longer show much interest.

Much of this sounds about as absurd as one of Louis XV's pronouncements. When he heard about a few miracles alleged to have taken place in a certain cemetery in Paris, he locked the cemetery gates and hung a sign on them that read: "By order of the King, God is hereby forbidden to work miracles in this place."[4] Even a king can't keep God from doing the supernatural, and he is foolish to try.

A comparable foolishness shows among shapers of opinion in contemporary Christianity. Under the pretense of rationality and modernity, an eagerness seems to be prevalent to deny or replace the supernatural. This damaging attitude adjusts the Gospels and Epistles according to the opinion of anyone who wakes up with a new notion, no matter how strange, heretical, or destructive it may be.

All this forces an answer to a pivotal question: when the supernatural has been abandoned, can the ministry actually be the ministry, and can the Church really be the Church?

Let me explain with an experience I had in London. I visited magnificent, historic Westminster Abbey, where I viewed acclaimed shrines, sat in the choir stall, walked near the crypts of famous people, and soaked up history. I en-

joyed an impressive worship service at the abbey with great
music and fascinating pageantry. Then I stood for 45 minutes
just outside the main entrance, where I watched hundreds of
tourists enter that magnificent monument to Christianity's
influence on Western civilization. I saw people enter and
leave with empty stares, who seemed to have no clue as to
the significance of the place. Like many modern churches,
Westminster Abbey had little meaning for many who came
there. But why be surprised? When the supernatural dimension is taken away, the church becomes just another social institution in the culture, a monument to help us celebrate our
religious traditions, or a cozy place to meet friends.

## BRING BACK THE POTENCY OF THE SUPERNATURAL

If vital Christianity is to impact this and coming generations, we must recover its supernatural potency. The purpose
and promise of what God intended the Church to be must revitalize our preaching, worship, pastoral care, and leadership. When the supernatural is restored, the church becomes
a meeting place with the holy God, who jars us into self-
judgment and beckons us to a radical reordering of individual, institutional, and spiritual priorities.

The supernatural, as observed earlier, is sometimes
within the range of human reasoning and sometimes beyond
it. I do not mean to imply that the supernatural is irrational.
But I do believe our finite reasoning abilities are not always
able to comprehend all God is doing. Like the law of gravity
or electricity or hydrogen energy, the supernatural exists
even when I do not fully understand it. Long ago Augustine
shed light on this issue: "Miracles do not happen in contradiction of nature, but in contradiction of what we know
about nature."[5]

Theologian J. I. Packer helpfully clarifies the creative
tension between the explainable and the unexplainable when
he reminds us, "God is as directly involved in the events that
we would not call miracles as He in those that we would describe as miracles."[6] A minister I know who has gone
through heartbreaking personal tragedy observed, "Every

act of grace, however small or great, is another miracle." The bottom line is that God wants to work supernaturally in our ministry, in His Church, and in His world, even when we cannot explain it or recognize it.

Our satisfying task, then, is to cherish and nourish "the Holy Involvement" rather than attempt to do God's work in our ability alone. New Testament scholar F. L. Godet illumines this issue when he says, "The miracles are visible emblems of what Jesus is and what He comes to do."[7] And I must add a contemporary dimension—and what He is doing now.

### SUPERNATURAL LESSONS FROM A WEDDING

To deepen our awareness of the supernatural, it's useful to ponder the first miracle of our Lord, at a wedding. Recall those wonderful words of the wedding ritual that are rooted in the old *Book of Common Prayer* that says Christ "adorned and beautified marriage by His presence and first miracle that He wrought, in Cana of Galilee." That powerful fragment of a sentence causes us to remember times when we celebrated weddings of friends, family, and neighbors—or even our own. And although the phrase points back to the first miracle, it also helps us see how Jesus provides a supernatural dimension in ordinary settings for average people with common needs. His first miracle created an extraordinary happening at an ordinary wedding reception. That's His pattern. He invades ordinary events and common circumstances wherever He is welcomed. We need our lives and churches permeated with such a God-nearness.

Picture the celebration at Cana, located just down the road from Jesus' hometown, Nazareth. As at most weddings, excitement ran high. Three generations of the bride's and bridegroom's families were probably present. Eccentric aunts and favorite uncles, destitute and affluent relatives, plus a generous sprinkling of first, second, third, and kissing cousins were likely there. A host of almost strangers also joined the guests for curiosity, wine, and food.

Children played noisy games near the reception area. Every teenage girl dreamed about her own wedding. From miles around, distant friends gathered along with the disciples of Jesus. And Mary—the wife of the carpenter and the mother of Jesus—was among the guests.

Jesus, as He blessed the boisterous event with His presence, tried to hear His mother's words above the happy commotion. She said, "They have no more wine" (John 2:3). She informed Him about a serious problem—no wine at a wedding was worse than no turkey, dressing, and sweet potatoes for Thanksgiving or no presents on Christmas. Something had to be done to save humiliation. And Jesus came through.

I love the contemporary application of this event made by a pastor in Appalachia. He preached four words from the account of this miracle with gusto—"They have no more!" He shouted, stomped, and planted his point into hearers' hearts as he preached about scarcity of the supernatural in the ministry of contemporary churches. He shouted, "They had no more wine, no more backup plans, no more morality, no more faith, no more expectancy, and no more miracles." The old preacher explained that the contemporary Church is weak, woebegone, impotent, desolate, and divided because it has forsaken the divine elements God intended to be part of her life. He believed this weakened state of Christianity comes from turning our back on the supernatural, giving up on miracles, and not intentionally seeking divine intervention in the details of church life. He insisted that God intends for His Church to be a showcase of supernatural happenings and human transformation. He insisted that a recovery of the supernatural would give the Church renewed authenticity and restored authority in the world. In the closing sentence of the sermon he insisted, "The supernatural is as necessary to the Church as oxygen is necessary for human life. We die without either!"

Considering the biblical summary the apostle John gives at the close of the wedding miracle account, the mountain preacher seems exactly on target. Remember the insightful summary? "This, the first of the miraculous signs, Jesus performed at Cana in Galilee. He thus revealed his glory, and *his disciples put their faith in him*" (John 2:11, emphasis added).

An impressive equation of grace is wrapped in that sentence: supernatural happening + revealed glory = increased faith by the disciples.

Evidently the Scripture writers thought the first miracle was designed to increase the faith of the disciples and to reveal the glory of the Lord as much as it was intended to produce fine wine for a wedding.

## HOW TO REDISCOVER THE SUPERNATURAL IN MINISTRY

Even a cursory reading of Scripture brings us face-to-face with supernatural events throughout the whole of redemptive history. Examining the miracles of the Bible sharpens our understanding of the importance of the supernatural in current ministry. And even though many of us are strong at suspicions and weak at believing, such a study shatters our doubts.

**1. Cultivate closeness to Jesus.** The supernatural always works better when we keep near Jesus. In the biblical record just before the wedding at Cana, He returned from the wilderness temptations. In the desert experience, He refused to turn stones into bread to feed himself, but now He turns water into wine to save His host from embarrassment.

In this record we see how Jesus' nearness makes ordinary events extraordinary. Who knows why He attended the wedding? But He did, and even though the wedding account is filled with excitement, enigma, and exhilaration, it is an event in which Jesus' presence made an incredible difference. That difference is needed in every expression of ministry in every congregation.

We always experience something supernatural when Jesus is present. It happens in many expressions of ministry—in baptism, in serving the Lord's Supper, in preaching the Word, or in singing in the choir. The Bible is right—when He is present and His glory is revealed, His disciples put increased faith in Him. Indeed, Scripture provides an unbroken record of how the Almighty works through those who keep close to Him.

**2. Practice unquestioned obedience.** The brief conversation between Jesus and His mother at the Cana wedding is interesting and deserves more study than we can give here. She wanted Him to help in a miraculous way, and He said He was not yet ready. It seems strange, then, that He proceeded to perform the miracle after saying, "Dear woman, why do you involve me? . . . My time has not yet come" (John 2:4). But He did.

In this process, the household servants at the wedding responded with almost blind obedience. Or maybe they were willing to do whatever Jesus' mother asked because of their desperate situation—"Do whatever he tells you" (v. 5). If your experience of weddings is like mine, you will understand that we might not expect Jesus to pay much attention to Mary. At most weddings, many motherly or fatherly types have an opinion about some detail, and to pay attention to all of them creates conflict and even chaos. But these servants listened and obeyed.

These servants followed exactly what seemed like bizarre directions. They were told to fill six jars with water, each holding 20 to 30 gallons, when they needed wine. Even though the request sounded like a departure from their highest priority, the result amazed them even as it does us: "You have saved the best till now" (v. 10).

**3. Use what you already have.** Jesus worked the miracle at the Cana wedding by using ordinary water, six stone jars, and familiar household servants. Every church has a supply of run-of-the-mill resources God will use.

Though I do not wish to overuse my imagination, could it be that in most churches the supernatural increases as God is allowed to invade and use existing resources to do a brand-new thing? If my supposition is true, then a greater use of what is already available may be more needed than new buildings, relocation of facilities, additional church members, a new church, or a different pastor.

**4. Expect extravagant results.** Jesus had baskets of leftovers at the feeding of the 5,000. While I am not sure what all this means for the contemporary Church, I do know Jesus Christ is a spendthrift when it comes to His gracious provisions for His Church. Low expectancy often produces low results, and extravagant expectancy often produces a bountiful harvest.

**5. Expect God to honor your best efforts.** The Church can never be all the Church God intended it to be without a supernatural element built into everything it does. Remember the old story about a farmer who received the commendation concerning his well-kept farm, "God has given you a remarkably beautiful farm," to which the farmer replied, "You should have seen it when He had it by himself." Of course, the story suggests God seldom does much without human help.

But try reversing the farmer's reply so that it relates to the modern Church. Regrettably, the Church in our time has reinvented herself into a human venture so we can say, "You should see the Church now that we have it alone."

Some contemporary churches have unnecessarily allowed themselves to become a heartbreaking empty shell of what God wants them to be. Today, as never before in human history, society needs a supernatural Church to be the agent of transformation for individuals and society—a living organism to accomplish God's mission in the world.

**6. Stretch your comfort zone.** Many supernatural happenings in Scripture forced people to risk new ways of thinking and stretch themselves beyond the status quo. The new birth called Nicodemus to think in new ways and to commit to new allegiances. In feeding the 5,000, Jesus used an obedient boy's lunch as the raw material for a miracle. I've always wondered what the boy thought when asked to give up his lunch and what he thought when he saw the results.

Or consider the stretching risks required of the persons Jesus healed on various Sabbath days: the impotent man at Jerusalem (John 5:1-9), the man born blind (9:1-14), the Capernaum demoniac (Mark 1:21-27), Peter's mother-in-law (vv. 29-31), the man with the withered hand (3:1-6), the bent-over woman (Luke 13:10-17), and the man with dropsy (14:1-6).

**7. Rethink how the supernatural could impact your church.** Consider how the supernatural impacts your understanding of prayer, Scripture, the scope of ministry, and your understandings of what the church is supposed to be.

Ask yourself the following questions: What effect would a sane emphasis on the supernatural have on the public worship services of the church? on the prayer efforts of the church? on the youth programs of the church? on nonbelievers who have shown some interest in the church? on your leadership team? on your family? on you?

Consider the impact a new emphasis on the supernatural would have on congregational renewal, on vision/mission, on motivation, and on your own personal renewal.

**8. Cultivate a supernatural perspective.** In discussing ways to fulfill the Great Commission in contemporary life, Bill Bright, founder and president of Campus Crusade for Christ, suggests a helpful seven-point strategy: (a) think supernaturally, (b) plan supernaturally, (c) pray supernaturally, (d) love supernaturally, (e) seek and use the supernatural enablement of the Holy Spirit, (f) believe God for supernatural results, and (g) become a part of the synergism of working with everyone who wants to fulfill the Great Commission in our times.[8]

## A SUPERB CREW IS NEVER ENOUGH

While sitting on a plane at Kansas City International Airport, waiting for the weather to clear so we could fly to St. Louis, the pilot took time to give us a pep talk over the public-address system. He said, "Even the superb flight and ground crew at Southwest Airlines can't fix the weather. Someone higher than us is in charge."

His speech gave me the capstone for this chapter. Even the most superb pastors, finest congregations, or most generous church budgets cannot take the place of the supernatural in the Church. And who would want to replace it with anything when we think of what Christ is prepared to do through His Church?

The supernatural work of Christ is a foundation of faith that underlies everything we try to do for the kingdom of God. It is the energy for fulfilling the mission of Christ in the world. It is the inspiration for much of the Church's ministry.

It is a source of faith to sustain us through every demand of ministry.

The Southwest Airlines pilot is right—"Someone higher than us is in charge." And that Someone works through us.

# 2

# Rediscovering a Holy Presence in Ministry

## Welcoming the Nearby God

It was a quiet Saturday afternoon at Florida's Broward General Hospital. As I completed my hospital calling, I hoped for an evening breather before Sunday. Having finished a grueling week, I felt too many people had needed too much of me during the last six days. Every pastor knows that feeling.

The hospital seemed unusually calm that day. Patients for Monday's surgeries had not yet been admitted. Doctors were off for the weekend, leaving sick people in the care of nurses and on-call physicians. Recovering patients had been released, so many rooms were empty. Visiting hours would not start for 30 minutes, so family and friends had not begun to arrive. The mood was unusually tranquil.

The serenity quickly changed with a page over the intercom: "Is there a pastor or priest in the hospital? Please call extension 226 immediately." I ignored the request at first. I thought, "Leave this to the hospital chaplain." I also rationalized that pastors from other churches must be calling on their sick members on Saturday afternoon, so they could respond. I argued to myself, "I can't look after the whole hospital. I don't want to get involved."

As the page persisted, I detected a desperate mood in the voice coming over the public-address system.

My inner Voice asked, "How long will you wait?" So I moved to a phone reluctantly. I was immediately connected with the emergency room supervisor. She informed me in anger, "A three-year-old boy has just died. He was brutally beaten. His stepfather is the prime suspect. Police are waiting outside the door to arrest the stepfather, who is here in the ER. It's an open-and-shut issue—this man is guilty as sin. I know it sounds preposterous, but he wants someone to pray with him before the cops take him away. And he *needs* prayer —he's a murderer."

Then she added quickly, "Pastor, everyone will understand if you don't come. Everyone in the ER hates child abusers. In our eyes, this stepfather is scum and trash."

As I forced myself to go, I experienced roller-coaster emotions. Even though I am a pastor, I hate murder and abuse. Never had I felt such hostility. The ER reeked with hate from the medical team, police, and family of the child. Meanwhile, I was asking myself many questions about trying to do ministry in such an antagonistic setting. I felt inadequate and confused.

I expected to feel all alone, but I didn't. Someone "like the Son of God" (Dan. 3:25, KJV) stood with me in the moment of great need when I stopped asking, "Why me?" A holy nearness was more real than my hands and feet. The mystery empowered me so that I could think, speak about forgiveness, and minister. That day I learned in a new way that the Presence means taking God into life—all of it. And it means ministry is always a duet and never a solo.

At Broward Hospital in the ER, this Helper from beyond made it seem that I was being guided by a supernatural automatic pilot. That day I experienced, in spite of my outrage and fear, something like what three Hebrew men felt when they were thrown into Nebuchadnezzar's fiery furnace. On second thought, maybe it was more like what Daniel experienced in the den of lions or what Elijah discovered among Baal's prophets on Mount Carmel.

## HOW THE PRESENCE ENRICHES MINISTRY

Wherever spiritual resources and ordinary life intersect, the Presence assures us that God is with us and He is for us.

Though the Presence is bigger than definition or description, let's consider how it enriches our service for Christ.

By the term Presence, I mean a God-nearness that is vivid, real, and affirming—as if the Almighty touched my hand or spoke an audible word. It is an awareness rooted in my own inadequacies that Someone makes me strong and effective. The Presence is as much for me as it is for those I serve, and it provides incredible joy, remarkable strength, and amazing staying power for ministry. It is akin to what William Wordsworth described as a "peculiar grace, a leading from above, a something given."[1]

### The Presence in Active Love

The "abiding center" that resourced me in emergency room 106 is what pastoral counseling pioneer Wayne Oates calls "the awestruck wordlessness."[2] Devotional writer Albert E. Day called it "the warm pervasive sweetness of ultimate reality—never completely out of call."[3] Still another writer, unnamed, depicts the Presence as the Helper who comes beside us in any expression of active love that we give in Jesus' name—a sympathetic word, a caring action, a trusting prayer, a thoughtful note, or a redemptive touch.

Awareness of the Presence comes in a special heart-to-heart moment when two human beings experience God together, so that they know two have become three, and the third is "like the Son of God."

### A Supernatural Connection

This Presence connects us to God so we can replicate the character of Jesus in our service for Him. His reliability, wholeness, and faith show up in us and our ministries. This holy nearness releases extraordinary expressions of compassion, increased spiritual savvy, authentic ways of seeing, empowered ways of being, and divinely energized ways of doing.

Presence has to do with taking God into chaos and painful alienation. It is an incarnational realization that Jesus is with us in ministry, and we know it. Parishioners recognize it too. And in the encounter, those who lead and those who follow are amazed and grateful that this association between them is more than friendship or a mere professional relationship.

This Presence radiates from ministering servants who are so totally open to God that the Almighty shows himself through their feeble human efforts. This Presence helps us continue the Kingdom work Jesus started during His earthly ministry, according to the promise "I tell you the truth, anyone who has faith in me will do what I have been doing. He will do even greater things than these" (John 14:12). It is an assuring awareness that an authentic ambassador of Christ never needs to carry out any facet of ministry alone.

Like the women at the empty tomb and the Emmaus disciples trudging along on their defeated homeward trek, this Presence provides a current resurrection in the midst of our despair, brokenness, and ambiguity. And this Christ-nearness never sees any reason to separate the secular and the spiritual, as we so often do.

## A Legacy from the Upper Room

Roman Catholic Bishop Fulton Sheen described the impact of the Presence on Christian service as being like a body exposing itself before the sun to absorb its rays.[4] And when we seriously consider the Presence, we see how accurate Sheen is—this near side of God is really like the sun that lights our way, warms our spirit, and develops our devotion and effectiveness.

Care and compassion sometimes takes the servant of Christ into the dregs of human life, where what he or she sees and feels may be shocking, untidy, untamed, or even miserable. This work makes us see people at their best and their worst. So we sometimes feel helpless and useless. And that is precisely what we are without the Presence.

But *with* the Presence, ministry becomes amazingly exciting work with eternal implications that are resourced by Resurrection power. Though the situation may appear to be no different with the Presence, we are different when He is near, and that makes everything else sparkle with meaning. The Presence means we can have the living Christ in our

ministry, as Leonard Griffith reminds us: "The promise of
His living presence was not just a bequest that Jesus made to
a handful of sorrowing disciples; it was an eternal legacy that
he bequeathed to his Church, the promise whereby he comes
into the world at all times and for all men who believe in him
as Saviour and Lord."[5]

## A WORLD CROWDED WITH GOD

Speaking of the Presence, C. S. Lewis wrote this striking
sentence: "The whole world is crowded with God." How incredibly true! Lewis continues with uncanny insight: "God
walks everywhere *incognito*. And this *incognito* is not always
hard to penetrate. The real labor is to remember, to pay attention. In fact, to come awake. Still more, to remain awake."[6]
Consider the rich possibilities of a "world crowded with
God."

This means every facet of ministry can be permeated
with Him. What an adventuresome partnership that provides for our ministry. So even when we foolishly try serving
in our own might with our own skills, God gloriously surprises us in unexpected places, at miraculous times, in extraordinary ways.

He becomes our Companion and our not so secret Source
for Kingdom endeavors. He reminds us of what we already
know—that no expression of service will ever be greater than
its source.

Every servant of Christ at some point in the journey
must decide what or whom his or her source will be. Will our
source be ordination, authority, education, family, reputation,
experience, church, or Christ himself? Every Christian leader
must decide to be a minister of Christ or a minister of the
church. Anyone can, of course, be a minister of the church
without Christ, but no one can be a genuine minister of
Christ without authentically impacting the church.

A Christ-resourced ministry has an incredible attraction
to those we serve, even when they may not fully understand
it or be able to explain it. But they respond nevertheless. They
know when they are in the presence of a Christ-saturated

Christian leader. Consequently, when the minister takes the Presence into the details of the ministry, he or she becomes a Christ-energized magnet to needy people. Leith Anderson is right: "People are looking for the supernatural. They may not know much about their denomination, or even their pastor. But they want to say, 'I can feel the presence of God there.'"[7]

Another divine serendipity follows—the Christian leader finds his or her work more satisfying and productive. Wayne Oates summarizes it well: "Not only does the Presence of God pervade all our relationships. Being near the Presence generates changes in us that make our being a 'presence' in our own right, as well."[8]

## MINISTRY AS MIDWIFERY

Newborn babies fascinate all of us, even though many of us probably know relatively little about the human birth process. Seasoned midwives experience great satisfaction in assisting at the birth of a child. Apparently, the fascination and satisfaction come from being able to see the results of helping another in time of need and in taking part in her experiences of creation.

Browne Barr applied this midwife metaphor to ministry in a story about a 16-year-old named Jim who loved his magnificent Siberian husky, Laska. When Laska started to birth a litter, Jim stayed by her side for most of a day and late into the night until the multiple births were finished. He protected, encouraged, and supported Laska in every way possible.

His assistance went well beyond professional service. After this experience with Laska, he had more than an intellectual notion about the birth process. In his wholehearted helping, Jim didn't think to hang out a shingle, print up business cards, or set up an appointment calendar for attending dogs at the birth of their puppies. Neither did he pontificate about the creation nor speculate about the Creator.

Instead, Jim did what love does—he showed compassion for Laska with tender actions. He persisted in expressing his affection for Laska. Barr reports the feelings behind the events: "When the night of Laska's labor was spent, Jim carefully shared her production with us. His eyes shone with the mystery of this moment of creation."[9]

The midwifery of ministry is much like that. Our eyes shine and our hearts skip a beat when we behold the transforming beauty of God at work in human personality. We are awestruck when we observe at close range the mysteries of grace. Ministry midwifery is serious, risky business, however, unless Someone coaches our efforts. In our own wisdom we don't know what to say or do. This nearby God always stands ready to assist. It is the holy Presence that says, "I will never leave you nor forsake you" (Josh. 1:5).

This midwife metaphor has limitations. The likeness, however, fits ministry in many ways, because the Christian leader's call allows the privilege of walking into people's problems uninvited and accompanied by the empowerment of God. So why go alone?

As Christ's representative, the servant of God encourages persons to recognize in every part of life that "God is here for you. Look up and take courage." So we share someone's pain in Jesus' name. Like a midwife, we know we cannot explain the pain away or deny the dilemma. Instead, we simply but redemptively take the Presence into the middle of the anguish. We stay close to those we serve. And as the holy Presence nourishes people through us, it is enough.

## How the Presence Makes Christian Serving Effective

The Presence is like some uninvited though welcomed guest. Think of the delightful way the Presence works through us in Christian service. For example, a minister calls in the hospital with nothing more than what appears to be a few friendly words—no medicine, no scalpel, no miracle drugs, and no medical credentials—but before he or she leaves, there is an encounter between God and the patient that is unique, special, and eternal. Charles Denison explains: "I am not to primarily assist the medical team or to interpret the crisis to the family. Far more important, my role is to humbly remind people caught up in crises or facing tragedy that God is present in their hour of need. I am not there to explain God or defend Him against the accusations of a grieving family; *I am merely there to point to His presence."*[10]

Something similar happens when ministry is offered in conversations, on a beach walk, on the phone, or across a restaurant table. It may hammer calloused hearts. Or it may come like a gentle spring breeze. It is God with us as we listen to eternity's whisper.[11]

Many contemporary servants of Christ, including me, are slow learners when it comes to grasping how limited our service is when done in mere human strength and cleverness. But when a troubling crisis forces us to recognize our limitations, we can welcome the availability, strength, and empowerment of "the nearby One."

This Presence is the unique factor a Christian leader brings to those he or she serves. Consider these eight principles for taking this supernatural dynamic into pastoral care and counseling.

**1. Never fear the Presence.** Though it is hard to acknowledge, some evade keeping close company with Jesus because of the demands He makes. Sometimes it is easier to be interested in causes and symptoms of problems than in cures or masteries Jesus offers. Some pastoral care and counseling spends more effort and time on analysis and diagnosis than on solutions. Sometimes God wants "yes" when we prefer to say "no." Sometimes the Spirit of Jesus tenderly reminds us of our inadequacies—that's humiliating business when we are feeling overly impressed with ourselves. Sometimes when we rush into our prayers, the Presence reminds us, "You have been dodging Me for days." God's nearness affirms and judges us.

C. S. Lewis underscores this corrective role of the Presence—"For God comes not only to raise up but to cast down; sometimes to deny, to rebuke and to interrupt."[12] The Presence can be demandingly radical when it questions our baser motives, our selfish pride, or our vain professionalism. Of course, we can be grateful that God sees behind our masks, image building, and love of prominence.

The Presence judges the Christian leader's intentions at the deepest levels. A. W. Tozer cautions,

> There is today no lack of Bible teachers to set forth correctly the principles of the doctrines of Christ, but too many of these seem satisfied to teach the fundamentals of the faith year after year, strangely unaware that there is in their ministry no manifest Presence, nor anything unusual in their personal lives. They minister constantly to believers who feel within their breasts a longing which their teaching simply does not satisfy.[13]

Though written more than a generation ago, those words are just as true today.

John Wesley's admonition about keeping close to the living Presence should also be considered: "Orthodoxy, or right opinion, is, at best, a very slender part of religion. Though right tempers cannot subsist without right opinions, yet right opinions may subsist without right tempers. There may be a right opinion of God without either love or one right temper toward Him. Satan is a proof of this."[14] Let's face the fact—unless the Presence is wonderfully obvious in us, our service for Christ has limited effect on those we serve.

All this means, of course, that the Presence may be neglected or even ignored because of His searching evaluation. The psalmist sings in 139:2-3, "Thou knowest me sitting or rising, my very thoughts thou readest from afar; walking or resting, I am scanned by thee, and all my life to thee lies open" (MOFFATT). How contemporary that word "scanned" sounds. The psalmist believes no circumstance, no situation, no hard place, no posture, no shift of time, no change of location keeps God from auditing the secret books of our soul.

On the surface, this searching aspect of the Presence sounds somewhat frightening. But several amazing benefits must also be recognized. Ministry efforts are continually under His care. The Presence means the Christian leader is never alone, is never out of God's sight or hearing. What assurance that brings for both our awesome and awful moments of ministry.

Think of the searching and strengthening available to us.

In the Old Testament God has "searched me and known me" (Ps. 139:1, NKJV), and the New Testament offers the strength that comes from the reality that Christ "loved me and gave himself for me" (Gal. 2:20). The Presence searches us, knows us, loves us, gives himself for us, and walks into every detail with us.

It is God who nourishes the soul, resources our ministry, and puts us at ease in His presence. He wants us to take delight in His nearby-ness. He welcomes our unconditional permission to walk into the details of our life and Christian service.

The psalmist removes all dread when he calls us to sing with the people of God, "Before a word is on my tongue you know it completely, O LORD. You hem me in—behind and before; you have laid your hand upon me. Such knowledge is too wonderful for me, too lofty for me to attain" (139:4-6).

In poetic language, former Methodist bishop Ralph Cushman once explained the attraction of the Presence:

> *There is a peace that passeth understanding;*
> *There is a joy the world can never know. . . .*
> *This joy of mine is not of earthly making,*
> *Though you may find it in the sunset's blush;*
> *Above the noise and din of human striving*
> *There is a Presence and a holy hush!*[15]

**2. Welcome the real Presence into pastoral care.** Effective pastoral care is in danger of becoming extinct. Arduous schedules, private living, and resurging individualism have thwarted redemptive relationships. Our own busyness, our preoccupation with lesser issues, and a near universal availability of psychological helpers in Western society also tend to undercut the practice of pastoral care.

However, our kind of frightening, confusing world requires that the care of souls be resuscitated and reenergized. Christ must become a recognized present Person rather than a dead Hero or the ancient Founder of Christianity. We must give theoretical notions about ministry a face and a heart—the face and heart of Jesus.

We must understand that as Christian leaders we represent the transcendent power of God—a power all people reach for in times of pressing need. We must take the Presence to individuals and to a society that desperately need God. We must be so saturated with intimate Christ-centered living that people see Him in us. This requires that we desert our professional pedestal and cast our lot with needy parishioners—to live out the spirit of Christ with them in their pain, problems, and victories too.

Where else can people go when life falls in? Or where *do* we go? In the dark valleys, more is needed than emotional adjustment, psychological soundness, or religious pep talks. People want God when their baby dies, when medical reports are bad, when jobs are lost, and when the unexplainable makes life desperate. This Presence is the real nearness of God that we take to hurting people.

Pastoral care is especially needed when the world is so full of crying and dying. The world needs more of the Presence now at the precise time when the Church and Christian leaders are preoccupied with debates between the right and left, liberals and conservatives, and traditionalists and contemporaries. People need Christ in the frightening dimensions of modern life. They hunger to see the Incarnation lived out in us. They want to know if this faith stuff works.

In troubled times like these, people need to know the living Lord identifies thoroughly with them; He sat where they sit and felt what they feel and suffered what they suffer. They especially look for a Christ-saturated leader whom they view as the only representative of God they can actually see.

Regrettably, pastoral care is too often neglected or viewed as a Lone Ranger responsibility by a pastor to a hurting individual or family. Nothing could be farther from the truth; we are not alone—far from it. There is Someone with us. We are privileged to take the holy Presence into every act of pastoral care, including ministry in crises, transition, victory, and even desperation.

By taking the nearby One into human need, the Christian leader becomes a faith formation specialist instead of a second-rate psychiatrist. Though servants of Christ may be well informed in the social sciences, their main task is to do what their personal faith journeys and biblical/theological understandings uniquely prepare them to do. In this process, they use spiritual remedies like prayer, Scripture, and Christ-centered relationships to cure souls. The Presence helps them do what they can do best. Their skills and remedies are not in competition with the treatment efforts of the psychologist or psychiatrist. The resources of the Christian leader are distinctive and even supernatural.

A faithful pastor friend, Rufus Beckum, in a personal letter, summarized this uniqueness from his own experience as

the strange, warm, comforting assurance of the nearness of God that may occur during counseling sessions where some great sin has been confessed and the lives and future of a family are at stake. Within my own reservoir of knowledge, I knew that I had no answer; but from somewhere deep in myself, the exact words flow from me, giving guidance and a possible solution to the problem. This has happened many times when in my total inadequacy to deal with a crisis situation, the answer has come.

**3. Sharpen awareness of the Presence.** Receptivity of the Presence comes through a blending of wholehearted aspiration and an appetite to be close to God. In spiritual shorthand language, this means practicing the Presence. Though Christ is everywhere, we often need to sharpen our awareness of His nearness. This is true of the Presence in Scripture, prayer, and worship; we must also watch for Him in persons and events. Nearness is a reality; awareness of nearness must be cultivated.

Receptivity requires us to actively welcome God into every phase of living, especially those places where we try to help others in His name and at those times when we represent Him. The demands of pastoral care, counseling, and soul friendship are times when the Presence is needed most.

One pastor who serves in the Midwest tells about taking five minutes for focused prayer before he begins any counseling session. He simply tells the counselee, "I need a few minutes of quiet preparation before we begin," and asks the person to wait outside his office. Sometimes he tells the counselee what he does during this time, and at other times it is a secret between God and himself. His typical prayer petition for the counseling event sounds like this: "Lord, this person I'm about to see needs more than I can give. I know You are more interested in this one's wholeness than I could ever be. Please help me to know what to suggest so he or she may be more like You. Open my mind to Your direction, and show me how to apply the Christian faith to this person's life."

A beginning Christian leader from another state, a member of "the new generation," tells how he initiates quiet talks with God in his car on his way to make hospital calls. He prays, "I'm new in ministry. I don't know what I'll face in this hospital room, but I need Your presence with me. Please give me Your heart for this situation and Your way of expressing it."

Although the songwriter is absolutely accurate to sing that God is as "close as the mention of His name," our awareness of the Presence can be increased by exercise. This Presence, however, is not an irresistible force God imposes on us. Rather, intentional listening and openness to Him are required to cultivate our capacity for connectedness with Him. Consequently, the Presence must be welcomed and cultivated if we are to realize its full usefulness.

Let's turn again to my correspondence with Pastor Beckum, who wrote,

It happened on August 29, 1987, when I received a phone call from a mother asking me to visit her son, a 29-year-old homosexual who was dying with AIDS. Quite honestly, I did not want to go. You remember the old mariners' motto, "We must go out, but we do not have to come back." That's how I felt, so I went.

After receiving the call, I went into the empty sanctuary and knelt at the front. I remember asking God to give me strength and courage and wisdom to do a job I did not want to do and did not know how to do. It was during that prayer that I received an assurance that He would go with me.

I felt impressed to take a small New Testament with me, even though I knew this young man was totally blind—a result of his illness. When I entered the home, I was ushered to the rear of the house to a small, cramped room where this young man lay dying. At that moment, I was aware of a supernatural Presence with me. I greeted this young man with a warm handshake and comforting words.

After we prayed and he assured me of his salvation, I baptized him. Then I placed the New Testament in his fevered hands, had a final prayer, and left.

Exactly one week later, I conducted his funeral. At that time, his mother told me he had held on to that little Testament and would not surrender it to anyone for any reason. I am so glad I went.

From that experience, I learned that the more dependent I am on God, the greater the reality I have of His presence.

Questions are easy to raise in such baffling circumstances, but why not rejoice that we as Christian leaders are given the privilege of representing the Father in such settings. And let's take courage from the fact that He promises to help us and always does when we listen carefully to what He wants us to say and do. He hears our hearts, and we hear His when we are tuned to Him. He answers when we pray with the psalmist,

> Light up my eyes with your presence;
> let me feel your love in my bones.
> Keep me from losing myself
> in ignorance and despair.[16]

**4. Cultivate the Presence to revitalize ministry.** Modernity sometimes takes ministry out of focus. Consider several examples. A pastor's visit to a parishioner's home can turn quickly into a friendly chat with very little spiritual verve or redemptive purpose. Hospital calls can be routine and sound a lot like an old country doctor who asks, "How you are feeling?" and "Would you like to go home soon?" Pastoral counseling can become like an office visit to a secular counselor who tries to uncover a thousand childhood difficulties without even considering conversion, prayer, spiritual accountability, or biblical insights as remedies. And a thousand voices, both inside and outside the Church, want to tell us what the Church's main purpose should be; as a result, the Church sometimes involves itself in everything from safe streets to gay rights to bowling leagues to welfare reform to Halloween alternatives to political elections. Could it be that our fuzzy focus is why many in the secular culture think the Church is irrelevant?

The weary outcomes of an overextended Church using secular strategies to help a dying world are not hard to find. They can be seen in empty lives, broken families, hollow religious highs, overdependence on science, and addiction to technology. We sometimes even see it in ministers who confuse their own ego needs with the Spirit's empowerment. To use biblical terms as found in Rev. 3:15, the contemporary Church is often "neither cold nor hot."

Seeking the Presence, however, keeps a church and her leaders on track. The Presence reminds us that neither individuals nor the world will be saved by bungling secular solutions brought into the Church. More money, more talk, more anger about victimization, and more effort invested in insignificant issues will not solve the moral bankruptcy of our time. Something more is needed. Theologian Thomas Oden calls for a refocus on our uniqueness and our opportunities: "Even seeming retrogressions sometimes offer gracious possibilities, as was the case with Noah, the Babylonian captivity, and Jonah. Biblically viewed, this cultural disintegration of our time is a providential judgment of sin and a grace-laden opportunity for listening to God."[17] Such a refocus provides a renewing intimate contact with the redemptive purposes of Christ.

We must continually remind ourselves that our weapons are essentially spiritual and supernatural. The apostle Paul puts these issues in clear perspective, and Eugene H. Peterson then puts the ideas in contemporary words: "The tools of our trade aren't for marketing or manipulation, but they are for demolishing that entire massively corrupt culture. We use our powerful God-tools for smashing warped philosophies, tearing down barriers erected against the truth of God, fitting every loose thought and emotion and impulse into the structure of life shaped by Christ" (2 Cor. 10:4-5, TM). The Presence helps us look past the problems to seize the possibilities of a Christ-shaped life.

Perhaps we need to build the insight of an African-American pastor into our ideas of ministry: "You white folks are interesting, because you meet to prove the existence of God. But we black folks come to experience the Presence."

**5. Cherish the Presence in the family of God.** The significance and power of relationships in Kingdom interests are deeper than the word "community" seems at first to imply. Our tender associations in the gospel are even more intimate and satisfying than the warm, meaningful phrase "the family of God" suggests. We need and thrive on fellowship that goes deeper than a meeting where our main props are Styrofoam cups, instant coffee, and sale-bought cookies.

Soul friendships and authentic fellowship in a spiritually healthy church offers everyone a nonjudgmental give-and-take environment where they can develop a great appreciation for the work God is doing in the character development of themselves and others. Then our hope for the world is rekindled by what we see in ourselves and in those close to us. Nearby trophies of grace encourage us to believe that God can do it over and over a million more times in individuals across the globe.

Judith Lechman, in her delightful book *The Spirituality of Gentleness*, details a lovely Quaker practice called "opportunities," which can best be described as the Presence moving through a group that had not met expressly for worship, something like a church business meeting or social gathering. "Opportunities" often take place when the group senses a desire from one or more persons to grow silent to hear the prompting of the Presence. Gradually all grow quiet, though no one apparently urged them to do so. Sometimes soft-spoken spontaneous petitions are prayed, or a short exhortation is given. The still focus continues until the "opportunity" seems to fade.

Think of the benefits for both individuals and churches. From her own experience of such events Lechman said,

"Every member of the group comes away with a new and often surprising sense of closeness, respect and understanding for others in the group. Refreshed by this unexpected movement of the Spirit, we see the world and our connection with God and our fellow humans within it from a perspective bordering on the sacramental."[18] Doesn't everyone and every group frequently need such an experience?

If growing deeper spiritual roots to produce more spiritual fruit is among the main purposes of the Church, then we must welcome the Presence to lead us into all truth, to give us a sense of belonging and accountability, and to nourish our souls. But more is available.

Even though pastor and persons in every congregation need all this, we know the power of the Presence goes beyond inner individual transformations. The Christian faith can also change the world. It has. And it will again. The early Christians, the Franciscans, the Quakers, and the Methodists are all examples.

In this effort to cherish the Presence, we need to expect to change our world—nearby and faraway too. Ask yourself what supernatural work needs to be done in your setting. I love the old story of the spiritually intense church that sponsored all-night prayer meetings asking God to permanently close the local tavern. One night, after being struck by lightning, the tavern burned to the ground. The owner sued the church for damages. Members of the church staunchly denied having anything to do with the fire. However, before dismissing the case, the judge observed, "Evidently the tavern owner had more confidence in the prayer of the church than the church members themselves had."

Let's think more radically about transforming our culture. Villages, towns, cities, counties, need to be impacted by biblical principles and renewed by incredible spiritual power that will challenge and revolutionize the existing moral, political, and social structures of our society. And it will be done by changing one person at a time.

**6. Allow the Presence to overcome your hesitations.** For years I have been moved whenever I dip into the insights of that remarkable world leader from another generation, Dag Hammarskjöld, who served as secretary-general of the United Nations. On Whitsunday 1961, he wrote in his journal titled *Markings*, "I don't know who—or what—put the question. I don't even remember answering. But at some moment I did answer Yes to Someone—or Something—and from that hour I was certain that existence is meaningful and that therefore my life in self-surrender had a goal. From that moment I have known what it means 'not to look back' and take 'no thought for the morrow.'"[19]

The Presence gave Hammarskjöld certainty that "existence is meaningful" and "my life in self-surrender had a goal." Doesn't every Christian leader, regardless of his or her setting of service, need an identical awareness? And when we possess those certainties, don't we automatically lose a thousand fears and frustrations?

In a thousand places contemporary Christian leaders are on hold. Some are afraid to attempt great things for God because the world has become too complicated. Others hesitate because they fear failure on their watch. Followed to its logical conclusion, hesitancy eventually shuts down ministry completely. To be spiritually viable, the Church has to be advancing without fear into the needy frontiers of contemporary society.

Recently I heard a highly placed Christian leader say, "I don't want to make a mistake, so I am overly cautious" When hesitations continue for months and years, the potentially harmful results must be considered. To do nothing is to accomplish nothing, and that undermines all the might-have-beens.

A veteran minister asked a rookie pastor about his hesitations when he knew what was right and what finally had to be done. The novice answered, "I'm afraid. Somebody won't like it if I initiate doing the principled thing."

The veteran replied, "What is the worst thing they can do to you?"

The beginner replied, "They could withdraw emotional and economic support from my ministry and cause me misery."

And the old hand answered, "They did worse to the Savior, but He refused to hesitate when He knew what had to be done."

This Kingdom leader's test of asking what is the worst someone can do puts many of our hesitations into proper perspective. In direct contrast, taking the Presence into ministry helps us know where to go, what to say, and how to say it.

Why not follow the process in Hammarskjöld's testimony: (1) listen for the decisive question from Someone or Something; (2) commit to your highest destiny—making a "yes" answer; and (3) stop the quivering debate inside yourself between the comfortable past and the threatening future.

Give up your hesitations about changing your world and get on with making a difference for Christ. More than ever before, inside the Church and outside in the world, leaders are needed with Christ-exalting insight, heroic devotion, and decisive action. Here's an action checklist:

- Preach what the Bible really says
- Become a radical Christian in civic issues
- Evangelize every class of people, including the upper-class
- Lead your church to live by biblical principles
- Relinquish your painful past
- Cultivate a soul friend or mentor
- Care for your own soul
- Share faith with everyone, including professionals
- Lead in absolute dependence on God

**7. Encounter the Presence in persons you serve.** My reminder for this idea comes from Mother Teresa and Tony Campolo, who found it in the teachings of our Lord: "Inasmuch as ye have done it unto one of the least of these my brethren, ye have done it unto me" (Matt. 25:40, KJV).

The idea is applied to our contemporary experiences in these colorful sentences from Tony Campolo: "God is a mystical presence waiting to be encountered in every person. He is in the fat lady, in the skinny man, in the oppressed black, in a difficult neighbor, in the male chauvinist, and in the downtrodden victim of the social system. In every one of them and in every other person I meet—my son, my daughter, my wife, my colleagues, and my friends—Jesus waits to be encountered."[20] Thus every relationship offers an opportunity to see our Lord—something like an old mine of spiritual potential in every meeting with another human being.

This looking for the Presence in everyone we serve takes dread out of ministry even as it transforms ministry into an adventure. Try it tomorrow as you start your day. See the face of our Lord in every person you meet, and see every problem person as a potential saint. Feel every heartache. Then duties will be transformed into delights of service offered in Jesus' name to the people He loves.

**8. Expect the Presence to make the ordinary significant.** Nothing like the Presence keeps us faithful at hard tasks in ordinary places. On a human basis, every ministerial assignment has at least 10 good reasons why the one assigned there should quit. Longtime pastors testify that every Sunday they have many good reasons to resign. On the contrary, every place is worthy of a leader who dreams big dreams for the Kingdom in that setting. What a quandary—what is a sensible person to do with a place that produces dread and at the same time stimulates dreams? It sounds contradictory, and it is.

However, in such a dilemma a pastor needs the Presence to help expect the unexpected, believe the unbelievable, and endure the unendurable. Face reality. The Presence knows where you are and what you need—God is fully aware of your limitations, your lack of confidants, your inexperience, and your childhood problems that sometimes hinder you.

The testimony of the spiritual giants in every century is that they always found enough light and enough energy for the next step. They reported that the Presence is always on time but seldom ahead of time. They unanimously agree that, beyond coincidence and their reasoning, they found a Guidance, a Companion, a Source, and a Confidant. He made it possible for them to accomplish great exploits for Him. Their achievements were based on a partnership with God. Their victories often came following old defeats.

Even as you read this page, you may be bewildered

about your Christian service assignment. Remember—God is never confused about you or your situation. One of God's delightfully amazing surprises is to transform all our liabilities, whether social, family, or economic, into incredible good for His kingdom.

Listen to this encouragement: About to enter his 88th year, and after having spent his entire life in service to Christ, Albert E. Day announced, "I cannot account for it all except by affirming that a Presence, not dependent on my moods nor baffled by the greatness of my need, has wrought a deliverance that is constantly transforming my life."[21] Such perseverance with grace is welcomed by everyone who tries to do ministry in any setting these days. The Presence is never baffled by our need or inexperience. The Presence keeps us at our post until the Commander in Chief reassigns us.

## THE POWERFUL PRESENCE—SUMMING IT UP

What benefit does the Presence give your service to Christ? Certainly not immunity to pain, brokenness, or adversaries. Throughout all human history, Christian service always involves God's call to come and die for the gospel. This Presence is an active awareness that works in partnership with the living Christ. It is a sense of standing in Christ's place, calling persons to miraculous reconciliation with God, themselves, and others. I like to think of it as "the shaping power of the indwelling Christ," to use Maxie Dunnam's phrase,[22] which gives nobility and importance to the church's service and to my own. In the presence of the King, my work is better, every system of body and brain is at full attention, and I am eager to please Him. My efforts are then more intensely motivated to distinctive service.

A moving welcome to the Presence is highlighted in Robert Wood's inspiring prayer:

Father God . . . Your presence is here

In the city—on the busy freeway, in the factory, in the cockpit of the airplane;

In the hospital—in the patient's room, in the intensive care unit, in the waiting room;

In the home—at dinner, in the bedroom, in the family work, at my workbench;

In the car—in the parking lot, at the stoplight.

Lord, reveal Your presence to me everywhere, and help
me become aware of Your presence each moment of
the day.

May Your presence fill the nonanswers, empty glances,
and lonely times in my life.

Amen.[23]

# 3

# Anointing— Empowered Speaking for God

## *How the Divine Speaks Through the Human*

When ministers get together, they usually talk about preaching. I heard a veteran minister say at a recent seminar, "Though I've preached about 2,000 sermons, anointing is a hard concept to explain. I know when I have it. And my parishioners know when I don't." Nervous laughter followed.

How to cultivate this supernatural element and factor it into preaching is a concern for every committed communicator of Scripture. Ministers chuckle sadly whenever they hear the old story about two typical church members who discussed the sermon as they left church. One asked the other, "What was the pastor talking about in his sermon?" The second worshiper answered, "I don't believe he said."

Across 2,000 years of Christian history, conscientious preachers have realized that authentic preaching demands more than mere human energy, mental sharpness, or competent speaking skills. This issue must have high priority for pastors, because supernatural passion in preaching sets the tone for all other phases of ministry in every church. Accordingly, preaching must have a holy touch and a divine approval if it is to achieve what God intends it to accomplish. Someone suggested that substantive sermons need at least three essential elements: (1) a great preacher, (2) a great theme, and (3) a great occasion. The supernatural resourcing of God on great preachers, great themes, and holy settings is what this chapter is about.

## CAN ANOINTING BE DEFINED?

Abiding values like love, loyalty, faith, hope, and mercy are difficult to discuss without being experienced. Anointing belongs on that wonderful list. It is joyful to experience, difficult to explain, and available to every preacher. Struggling to explain anointing, a beginning preacher called it "an incredible turn-on where thinking, faith, feelings, devotion, and responsibility meet."

Having his own difficulty with definition, a seminary professor suggests anointed sermons are something like a sacrament, where God uses ordinary stuff to accomplish supernatural results. The instructor went on to argue what we already know—every preacher is as ordinary as bread in Communion and water in baptism. The professor was embarrassingly accurate about our ordinariness.

An experienced preacher-pastor insisted preaching has little worth or meaning until it is heard redemptively as a message to the gathered people of God from their heavenly King. In this view, preaching does not actually become preaching until it produces a responsive hearing among active listeners.

All who have ever preached know anointing grips a preacher's mind and stimulates the emotions. But there is more beyond this obvious impact, because anointing toughens, questions, and strengthens the preacher's entire being for the task of speaking reliably for God.

A British preacher, Martyn Lloyd-Jones, explains how to cultivate this anointing: "Seek Him! Seek Him always. But go beyond seeking Him; expect Him. Do you expect anything to happen to you when you get up to preach? . . . Seek this power, expect this power, yearn for this power; and when this power comes, yield to Him. Do not resist. Forget all about your sermon if necessary. Let Him loose you, let Him manifest His power in you and through you."[1]

## Authentic Anointing Develops New Insights

Anointed preaching always centers on Christ and clarifies our words about Him. Unction enhances the awareness of Jesus that is already partially present in the sermon study, brought there by our experience, character, and commitment. Authentic anointing provides a direction for the sermon and makes us aware of a holy approval. This approving relationship is something like a father's cheer at a Little League baseball game, or a mother's loving word as her child leaves for school, or parents' proud affirmation at their child's college graduation. Anointing assures preachers that they have divine approval.

Unction increases insight, clarifies toil in the study, and focuses energy. This God-nearness makes a preacher stand at full attention, ready to deliver his or her soul with a full assurance of being in sync with God. One preacher calls unction a Spirit-directed way of knowing.[2] To sharpen our thinking about these supernatural dimensions of preaching, we must recognize that anointed preaching means to know what God wants said to a particular people in a specific setting at a given time.

## Authentic Anointing Requires a Holy Encounter

Anointing or unction starts with a holy encounter with God in a scriptural passage that makes a visceral claim on a preacher's personhood, readiness, preparation, sermon delivery, and emotions. It questions the minister's piety, pride, and purity. G. Campbell Morgan once observed about this holy encounter: "Formerly it was said that a preacher was to 'handle his text.' But when a text handles the preacher, it grips and masters and possesses him, and he is responsive to the things he is declaring, having conviction of the supremacy of truth and having experienced the power of truth. I think that is what most produces passion for preaching."[3]

Such an encounter with Scripture makes a preacher stretch for thoughts and search for words to express what

God wants done. Unction infiltrates and illuminates the preacher's toil with word meanings, exegesis, contexts, propositions, structures, and creativity. Anointing is the sun at high noon enlightening every part of preaching.

A holy anointing does more than improve a sermon's delivery—it makes us aware that God saturates the whole sermon development and delivery effort. Spurgeon offers a lovely idea when he suggests that a part of anointing is the art of rightly using what we know.[4] Such a holy anointing never results from merely seeking to have something to say or from checking a lectionary to see what others will preach on a given date. Martyn Lloyd-Jones was right: "To me there is nothing more terrible for a preacher, than to be in the pulpit alone, without the conscious smile of God."[5] Thus it may not be an overstatement to say that preaching without encounter is not authentic preaching.

To help us understand this holy encounter, E. M. Bounds quotes an old Scottish preacher: "There is sometimes something in preaching that cannot be ascribed either to matter or expression, and cannot be described by what it is, or from whence it cometh, but with a sweet violence it pierceth into the heart and affections and comes immediately from the Lord."[6] That's it—anointing is God's way of empowering a frail human being to speak adequately or even supernaturally for Him.

### Anointing Ignites a Holy Fire

Lots of contemporary preaching is technically good with little passion. Let's be clear—sparks of anointing may be ignited at any point along the way in sermon preparation or delivery. But it must be ignited somewhere. London's City Temple Pastor Joseph Parker of a past generation was absolutely accurate in his strong statement "It is fire that makes a difference between one preacher and another; it is not intelligence or the mere use of the right words."[7]

Samuel Shoemaker, gifted Episcopalian pastor and founder of Alcoholics Anonymous, advised preachers that this fire is needed so we may hear God "say fresh, vivid, exciting, moving and convincing things through us . . . so that there is fire in us that leaps from Him to us and from us to them."[8]

## GENUINE ANOINTING IS SUPERNATURAL

From a mere human point of view, preaching is absurd. Think how it works, when it works. The preaching process supposes that an otherwise flawed human being speaks for God to a contemporary congregation. His or her modern message must be rooted in a 3,000-plus-year-old Book handed down from antiquity. Preaching presumes that an average common human being—the preacher—can accurately hear the Almighty so well as to pass on a fresh, life-giving word to the people. The anointed preacher feels obligated to offer an important word that can change a listener's life forever, as it often does.

Every preacher asks, some every day, "How can a mere human being like me fulfill such lofty expectations?"

### A "Foolish" Strategy

The apostle Paul, to make sure no one misunderstood these unbelievable realities, announced that God planned to save people through the "foolish" strategy of "preaching" (1 Cor. 1:21, KJV). The secret is a divine anointing that transforms a foolish-appearing and incredibly complicated human communication process into a redemptive event.

Anointing produces a certainty in the preacher's mind that preaching is more than a human-initiated, self-centered oration. This unction makes preaching a supernatural communication event that brings authority and fervor and insight to the preacher so he or she is enabled to proclaim the good news of what God is doing through Christ at the present moment.

Let's be more specific. What, then, is anointing for preaching? It is allowing oneself to become a supernatural spokesman to speak for God to human needs around us. Or to say it more precisely, anointed preaching happens at the intersection at which the Spirit of God, the Word of God, the preacher, the message, the hearers, the human needs, and the setting all connect.

### The Supernatural Foundation

Real anointing demands that a preacher allow the meaning of a biblical passage into the intricacy of his or her own thoughts and character. Before preaching a passage or truth, the preacher must allow Scripture to scrutinize personal sensitivities, suspect inner motives, strengthen intrinsic weaknesses, and question his or her pride. This passionate realization of the Almighty speaking to the preacher through a biblical passage helps the minister of the Word get ready to preach with the awe and amazement that he or she is trusted to be a spokesperson for God.

Authentic anointing most often starts with musing, discovery, engagement, imagination, involvement, soul-searching, reflection, personal spiritual stretching, and a willingness to be personally shaped by a biblical truth. Anointing, the real kind, often nags and pesters and questions and blesses the preacher long before the sermon is preached. It may wake the spokesperson at night or make him or her anxious about personal worthiness to speak before stepping behind the pulpit. As God's anointed spokespersons, we are given opportunity to point people to the sunburst of the gospel in the middle of the blackest storms of contemporary culture. That requires that a preacher know a lot about both sunshine and darkness.

### The Urgency Factor

Authentic anointing makes a preacher anxious about the spiritual condition of all who hear the preaching. Every contemporary pulpiteer should seriously consider these five sentences written by Richard Busch: "The Holy Spirit will move them [the hearers] by first moving you. If you can rest without their being saved, they will rest, too. But if you are filled with agony for them, if you cannot bear that they should be lost, you will find that they are uneasy, too. I hope that you will dream about your hearers perishing for lack of Christ and begin to cry, 'O God, give me converts or I die.' Then you will have converts."[9]

### Personal Spirituality Demanded

Anointing necessitates a creative engagement and an honest, accountable connection with holy resources. The issue for the preacher is to keep the soul warm and tender toward God. The minister must be joyously intimate with Christ so this close connection shapes the thought and life. G. Campbell Morgan insisted two generations ago, "Truth and life travel together in the preacher's preaching."[10] Christ Jesus himself is our inspirational Example of the combination of spiritual power and ultimate truth in human form.

An insightful listener remarked to Scottish preacher Alexander Whyte, "Today you preached as if you had come straight from the Presence."

Whyte answered shyly, "Perhaps I did."

That's the important issue. Even though intimacy with Christ is seldom discussed in relationship to preaching, it is the beyond-doubt secret of spiritual passion in proclamation.

Anointing unites the holy presence of God and the human frailty of the preacher so he or she is able to speak insightfully and inspirationally for "the Holy Other." God's strength and human weakness meet in an anointed sermon, so the preacher sings with the whole heart during the entire sermon preparation and delivery process, "Now let the weak say, 'I am strong.'"

This personal spirituality experience component is the opposite of what I sometimes see in my preaching students. When such a situation arises, I say, "Your sermon is biblical and well prepared, but your eyes show nobody is at home in your heart." Too many of us try to preach with well-furnished minds but empty hearts. Years ago unction and passion and anointing were so absent in one American frontier preacher that the Indian chief insightfully remarked, "Big thunder, no rain." Sad but true, the pioneer's descendants still live among us—in fact, we may be some of them.

Writer Gary Thomas offers a challenge to preachers to care and cultivate personal spirituality:

> The church has lost much of its authority to address the slide into the moral morass because some of our pastors have produced lives that make them candidates for TV talk shows. I think we need a new revolution. . . . I'm tired of hearing about how "inspired" a new preacher is, of what

new spiritual manifestation is coming down from heaven. Instead, I want to see character. I want to see men who have made the hard moral decisions and thus have embodied the excellence of the Christian faith. I want to hear about people who have made every effort to add to their faith goodness.[11]

## Produces Clear Speech

Genuine anointing shows we are so intimately acquainted with God and awed by Him that we diligently try to apply biblical truth accurately to our times, our churches, and ourselves. A passion for preaching always helps us speak clearly and plainly. Many preachers need to think through this connection between anointing and plain, clear thinking and speaking. God never inspires garbled pulpit speech.

Joe Bayley states the issue conclusively with this story: "Graffiti scrawled on a wall at a university read, 'Jesus said to them, "Who do you say that I am?"' And someone had written in reply, 'You are the eschatological manifestation of the ground of our being, the kerygma in which we find the ultimate meaning of our interpersonal relationships.' And Jesus said, 'What?'" Bayley continues, "Our Lord was profound, but simple in expression. Ordinary people heard Him gladly, eagerly. To use an old but true way of expressing it, He put the cookies—or the bread of life—on the lowest shelf where anyone could reach it. And so must I."[12]

To have unction in preaching requires that a preacher genuinely understand the gospel and have a fiery passion for it. With a word of apology to author John Stapleton for a bit of editing, his stalwart sentence summarizes the spiritual dynamics of preaching: "Passion lifts up the right words in the right order and sends them forth from the preacher on wings of sound as a message from the speaking God to the listening people."[13]

## UNCTION STARTS WITH SCRIPTURAL SATURATION

Wrestling with the message and meaning of a scriptural passage is where anointing originates; the sermon, without this Bible saturation, lacks soul passion and has little meaning to hearers. Dennis F. Kinlaw, Old Testament scholar, evangelist, and former president of Asbury College, himself an exemplary model of anointed preaching, helpfully explains the important place of the Bible as our Source for unction in proclamation.

In Kinlaw's 1984 preaching lectures at the Billy Graham Center at Wheaton College, he recounted his student days at Princeton when Old Testament scholar Otto Piper remarked in class,

> You know, young men and young ladies, many people feel that Calvin and Luther produced the Reformation. But it wasn't Calvin and Luther. What happened was that when Luther read the Book of Galatians, he listened; and when he listened, it exploded inside him; and when the truth of Galatians exploded inside him, he didn't have any better sense than to go tell it to other people! A similar thing happened with Calvin. Calvin's congregation knew what he was going to preach on a given Sunday because he simply started with the verses following the one where he quit the previous Sunday.[14]

Such an explosion of the meaning of Scripture is needed in every congregation, especially in our period of human history.

Regrettably, a serious setback occurred somewhere along the line of church history. Piper described the detour: "The great tragedy of the Reformation was that when Luther died, Melanchthon edited his work. And when Calvin died, Beza edited his work. Melanchthon encouraged the people of Germany to read the Bible to find Luther's doctrine in it, while Beza encouraged the people of Geneva to read the Bible to find Calvin's doctrine."[15] There is an important lesson here for us. A preacher who seeks anointing does not read the Bible to find something to say, but to be personally found by the truth of Scripture.

### God's Message for the Preacher

Well-known veteran African-American pastor Gardner C. Taylor, who impacted Brooklyn through 30 years of preaching at Concord Baptist Church, reminds us with powerful language: "The magnificent anomaly of preaching is to be found in the fact that the person who preaches is in need himself or herself of the message which the preacher believes he or she is ordained to utter." Then Taylor adds this forceful question that demands our answer: "How dare such a person address others, in the name of God, who are no worse off than the spokesman?" He continues, "This is almost incredible presumptuousness which ought to prompt every preacher to pray with anguish and bewilderment in the spirit of the words of the song of my own forebears, 'It ain't my brother and it ain't my sister, but it's me, O Lord, standin' in the need of prayer.'"[16] All this is growing confirmation that the starting point for anointing begins when the preacher sees how the Bible intimately exposes oneself to one's own gaze while waiting before God. The result is spiritual self-discovery—a missing ingredient in much of contemporary preaching.

As everyone knows, anointing is inescapably connected to a preacher's fidelity and honor and faith. In preaching, the real person shows, whether a preacher knows it or not. The minister engages in self-revelation when opening his or her mouth in the pulpit.

Since every preacher reads the Scriptures and sees the world from a personal vantage point, the preacher needs to submit to as many accurate reality tests as can be found. Such a test of reality was posted on the vestry wall in an Aberdeen, Scotland, church. Its purpose was to confront every preacher as he mounted the pulpit stairs. The plaque read, "No one can both glorify Christ and himself at the same time."[17] A similar placard in blazing letters might be beneficial in pulpits everywhere.

Such a reality becomes a preacher's spiritual serendipity while preparing to preach. Kinlaw offers this forceful insight about the self-discovery aspect: "We must present the Bible not only as the Word of God, but as the Word of God about us. . . . That can occur only through the enlightening power of the Holy Spirit. Then, when the Spirit's internal revelation breaks into the preacher's mind and attends his preaching, it has the potential for radically transforming people's lives."[18]

At this present moment, the greatest need for supernatural preaching power is for every preacher to authentically hear what Scripture says personally so that others can be told about the discovery. Only as God's Word permeates a preacher's life does a holy anointing become available in the sermons that follow.

**Cure for Deadly Dullness**

Remember Eutychus, the New Testament man who fell asleep during one of Paul's long sermons? David H. C. Read, longtime former pastor of Manhattan's Fifth Avenue Presbyterian Church, in a charming magazine article once discussed what makes preaching interesting. He suggested we can keep contemporary Eutychus from feeling toxic boredom by communicating the mental excitement of personally encountering the Word of God. After a paragraph decrying dry dullness, Read observes, "The trouble with ministers, missionaries, and church workers is that they are always meeting and talking with ministers, missionaries, and church workers."[19] How incredibly correct. Too often, we use an inside vocabulary to try to reach an outside world. Why choose the dullness that comes from talking too much to ourselves when we could enjoy and share the spiritual excitement of Scripture with the people who hear us preach?

Unction, then, produces a growing awareness for a preacher that there need not be boredom if the minister has come fresh from the Presence. Such freshness comes from internal preparation—prayer, meditation, and waiting on God. The ensuing anointing makes a sermon into a message. Then the Spirit of God actually transforms the preaching into an event in which the grace of God impacts the people.

## UNCTION COSTS PLENTY

Anointing in preaching, even though it is a gift from God, is costly business, expensive in effort and faithfulness. Anointing requires a lifelong resolution to be an effective preacher. It costs commitment and dedication to speak usefully for God. Divine anointing begins with holy living by the preacher, and that costs much in devotion and duty to Kingdom priorities.

Anointing demands spiritual preparation for a particular preaching event. One powerfully effective preacher I know spends the last two hours before each preaching event soaking in the message; it is no surprise that he seldom preaches without a sense of holy unction. Princeton's Andrew Blackwood, sometimes called the dean of preachers of his generation, addressed this issue insightfully: "The biblical sermon is likely to be worth as much or as little as it costs in time and thought, in work and prayer. In his study, the prophet can build his altar and lay the wood on it. There he can lovingly place his sacrifice—the waiting sermon. All of this he is glad to do as well as he can, but still the fire must come from God. Come the fires will, if he prays before he works, and if he works in the spirit of prayer."[20]

Concerning the cost of unction, Douglas Bennett, professor at Southern College in Collegedale, Tennessee, insists, "Spirit-anointed preaching does not come without our being willing to pay a great price—that of being broken by God, molded by prayer and prostrated in humble dependence upon God for power."[21]

The Lord's anointing is seldom given to one who has given little effort to preparation. I say "seldom" because I believe God sometimes takes pity on congregations whose pastors refuse to pay the price for anointing; then God gives blessed utterance to their pastor for the people's sake and not for the pastor's. Too much contemporary preaching uses mere human resources, and it produces mere human results. God always allows us to preach without anointing if that's our desire. But why preach in human strength, however gifted you may be, when you can have divine empowerment?

Try paying the extravagant price of powerful preaching with prayer, personal spiritual formation, brokenness, and fasting. Then you will have the anointing. Though this commitment demands energy, produces humility, and makes us totally dependent on God, the resulting anointing is well worth any price.

# 4

# Preaching—
# the Miraculous and
# Audacious Meet

## Proclamation Insights from
## Mentors and Fellow Strugglers

Every preacher has been impacted by mentors without knowing what to call them. For generations preachers have learned their craft by listening, watching, reading, trying, and preaching—all difficult to do without help from a mentor, caring pastor, or father or mother in the faith.

My pivotal preaching mentors were ministers whom readers would not know or might not desire to know. But they impacted me greatly. I can't forget them, and I don't want to. Some never knew how they affected me because I was too shy to tell them, and the few times I mustered courage to tell others, they didn't know how to handle my admiration.

One of my mentors—and I had several—taught me to pray, another taught me spiritual passion, another love for Scripture, another exegetical strategies, another about pastoral caring, another about authenticity, another about sermon delivery, and another about personal piety. I never preach without realizing that my mentors are somehow present in my preaching. They cheer me on like the biblical "cloud of witnesses" (Heb. 12:1). They assure me, affirm me, and correct me. They remind me that holy anointing can be fun and provide fulfillment for preacher and hearers alike. And you have enjoyed similar personal growth experiences made possible by your mentors.

Accordingly, I wanted to add a mentoring dimension to this discussion of the supernatural aspects of preaching. I wanted to think again about what mentors and colleagues believe about anointing. I wanted them to mentor this discussion of the nonspectacular supernatural elements of ministry. So I invited several old friends into this discussion.

## WHAT AN OLD PREACHER
## TAUGHT ME ABOUT ANOINTING

E. M. Bounds mentored me, though he lived generations earlier. I was impacted forever as a student minister by his book *Preacher and Prayer.* Soon after I acknowledged a call to ministry, my fathers in the faith encouraged me to read Bounds. And I am glad they did, because he underscored the spiritual dynamic of the work of ministry for me. Contemporizing the language a bit, here is what Bounds taught me:

• Unction does not come by effort, eloquence, or ordination.

• Unction distinguishes preaching from other speech.

• Unction and earnestness and noise can be naively confused.

• Unction permeates revealed truth with the energy of God.

• Unction inspires and clarifies a preacher's intellect.

• Unction gives insight, grasp, and projecting power.

• Unction generates heart power as well as head power.

• Unction makes preaching sharp to those who need sharpness.

• Unction is like a fresh morning dew to those who need refreshment.

• Unction is kindled by continuous prayer.

• Unction takes the Word of God to listeners in different ways according to their need—sometimes like dynamite or salt or sugar.

• Unction suffuses, softens, percolates, cuts, and soothes.[1]

## WHAT YESTERDAY'S GIANTS BELIEVED ABOUT ANOINTING

The supernatural need for anointing—the need to hear another voice—is much more evident in preaching literature from the past than in the present. Perhaps present authors assume it is present, or perhaps they do not see its importance. Published material about preaching from previous generations is filled with discussion about this supernatural need for all of preaching. Let's examine several examples from the past for our present instruction.

• **Jonathan Edwards: "An anointing grace."** Trying to explain unction, Jonathan Edwards suggested, "Our people do not so much need to have their heads stored, as to have their hearts touched."[2]

In a biography of Edwards, Ralph Turnbull observed about the Northhampton preacher: "We do well to recognize that there rests upon select messengers of God an unction of the Holy One, an anointing grace, a mysterious extra which melts and burns by its fiery baptism. That was Edwards's secret. He who preferred to write the message was constrained to speak mightily as borne along by the divine Spirit."[3] Great insight! But we challenge Turnbull with the question, "Do you truly think anointing rests only upon select messengers of God, or is it for all preachers?"

• **Charles Spurgeon: "Every faculty . . . joyously excited."** No growing preacher wants to forget the wisdom of this paragraph from Charles Spurgeon:

> From the beginning of the sermon to the end we might at times say, "Whether in the body or out of the body I cannot tell: God knoweth." In anointing everything has been forgotten but the one all-engrossing subject in hand. If I were forbidden to enter heaven, but were permitted to select my state for all eternity, I should choose to be as I sometimes feel in preaching the gospel. Heaven is foreshadowed in such a state: the mind shut out from all dis-

turbing influences, adoring the majestic and consciously present God, every faculty aroused and joyously excited to its utmost capability. Then all the thoughts and powers of the soul are joyously occupied in contemplating the glory of the Lord, and extolling to listening crowds the Beloved of our soul. And all the while the purest conceivable benevolence towards one's fellow creatures urging the heart to plead with them on God's behalf—what state of mind can rival this? Alas, we have sometimes reached this ideal, but we cannot always maintain it, for we know also what it is to preach in chains, or beat the air.[4]

Spurgeon recommended that we must pray while we preach to receive and maintain anointing.[5]

• **Augustine: "Catch the affections."** Augustine spoke of anointing "to inform the understanding, catch the affections, and hence the will of his hearers."[6]

• **Richard Baxter: "A son of thunder."** Seventeenth-century nonconformist Richard Baxter said of anointed preaching, "Sometimes, one arises in difficult times, or in fermenting times, a son of thunder, that looks all enemies in the face, and volunteers a defiance even when it would have been easy to evade it."[7] Our times and circumstances could use that kind of unction now.

Of his own preaching Baxter said in another setting, "I preached as never sure to preach again, and as a dying man to dying men."[8] Every preacher who makes that affirmation just before starting to the pulpit might be surprised by the anointing he or she would experience.

C. R. Brown, in his 1923 Yale lectures, said of Baxter's anointing: "This man got his power by being alone with God and by looking into the face of God! And it is there we get our power too. There is no substitute for this power and no other way of getting it. It is the soul that has caught fire from the altar which sets other souls on fire."[9]

• **John Henry Jowett: "Mysterious impressiveness."** In his 1912 Yale lectures, John Henry Jowett noted what happens when anointing is missing: "Our speech lacks a mysterious impressiveness. We are wordy but not mighty. We are eloquent but not persuasive."[10]

• **Phillips Brooks: Christ centered.** Like us, Phillips Brooks, a Boston pastor from another era, experienced difficulty in defining unction, so he piled words upon words like enthusiasm, eloquence, magnetism, or the gift of preaching. Brooks, however, must have intimately demonstrated the anointing. Members of his church who heard his preaching erected a monument to his memory that stands to this day in the courtyard of Boston's Trinity Church. The statue shows Brooks in his pulpit, and a figure of Christ stands beside him with His hand resting on the preacher's shoulder. What a tangible tribute to anointing! The sculptor, who thoroughly studied the Boston pastor in order to create the statue, said one could not explain Brooks apart from his relationship to Christ.

• **Donald G. Miller: "More than the sum total of the parts."** In discussing supernaturally intangible qualities of proclamation, Donald G. Miller wrote in his epic book *The Way to Biblical Preaching,*

> anointing is that elusive quality of either spoken or written discourse which gives tone and texture and catches up the listener into a world created by the truth which becomes for the moment, at least, more real than the world of time and sense. It is an intangible quality—perhaps more tinged with imagination than with logic—which determines mood and reaches the deeps of the whole person. . . . It is reason, feeling, volition, in combination with an indefinable residue of reality which is vastly more than the sum total of each taken separately.[11]

• **W. E. Sangster: Makes preaching distinctive.** British Methodist pastor W. E. Sangster, himself a published respected homiletician, observed how anointing makes preaching distinctive: "One thing which distinguishes preaching from all other forms of public speaking is that preaching can have unction. That we have it so rarely is the sadness of us preachers and proves the poverty of our prayers."[12]

Dip into preaching literature in any generation, and you find anointing was understood to mean that God becomes a yokemate with a minister in the preaching. Then through this blessed anointing, the Almighty does incredible things through an ordinary individual who keeps open to God. All this dynamic in preaching creates a growing awareness that we are called by God, resourced by God, and assigned by God to serve spiritual needs of a given group of people.

## WHAT COLLEAGUES SAY ABOUT ANOINTING

Though homiletical literature from past generations speaks convincingly about the desirability of anointing, I wondered what contemporary preachers were thinking about this supernatural component of proclamation. So I wrote several preacher colleagues, asking them to tell me what anointing meant to them.

### Eventfulness—More than Preparation

In a letter, Pastor Carl Green recalls extraordinary times when his congregation experienced a holy presence in his preaching—so unusual that he decided to relisten to the sermon on audiotape. But when he listened, he was sorry: "It was not the same—the divine electricity was missing. Evidently Memorex tapes can't capture anointing!"

In another paragraph Green discusses "the elusive, real, but difficult to define unction and anointing" as a necessity for preaching that goes beyond thorough preparation. He believes when we are "empty of this forceful life of the Spirit in preaching," we are left with merely good preparation and good delivery and good stuff. But mere good stuff is never good enough for God or His people.

### God's Pleasure Inspires

Pastor Dan Boone of the Olivet University Church in Kankakee, Illinois, states in a letter, "Anointing is a sense of confidence in preaching, confronting, and leading that comes at the time the task is being carried out." He then offers this unique insight: "More than anything the components of anointing or unction are the knowledge that God is pleased with what I am doing, and His pleasure inspires; and it is an awareness that others have interceded for me and are expectant."

When asked to recount a special personal experience of anointing, Boone's example demonstrates that the supernatural is not always spectacular. He wrote, "Recently I confessed a sense of spiritual dryness to my Wednesday night Wesley cell group. They laid hands on me and prayed simply and directly that I might receive a fresh anointing. Sunday, though I had almost forgotten our prayer time, in the midst of preaching I sensed a boldness, a confidence, and a dynamic work of the Spirit in myself and among the people. The anointing left me humbled and broken rather than emotionally charged."

### Anointing Activated by Prayer

Veteran Pastor Roy A. Litsey wrote that anointing/unction is elusive, but "I definitely know when I have it, and it seems I am more aware of anointing when I am well prepared—exegetically and spiritually." He also discovers and appreciates a two-way interaction of blessing on his preaching as a result of the intercession of persons in his congregation. With gratitude he observes, "Many people in my present congregation are great people of prayer. I would guess that this is the real reason they are telling me that my preaching in recent months has greater depth and more inspiration. Their prayers help them and me enjoy God's anointing on my pulpit efforts."

### Anointing Sometimes Comes as "Interruptions"

Pastor Michael Benson, son of itinerant preacher and author Bob Benson, describes formative concepts about anointing from his early days in ministry. After explaining that he was raised with a sacramental view of life, he wrote, "Early in my pastorates I literally held the view that Sunday morning and evening were the times of proclamation, and most other tasks were interruptions. I labored under the delusion that I had to have 20 hours of preparation to be worthy of the Lord's anointing."

Always a restless pilgrim, now serving as an itinerant evangelist and conference speaker, Michael continued in his letter,

Being shaped by Henri Nouwen's idea that interruptions are our work, I see now that the work of being a pastor offers numerous opportunities for proclamation outside the Sunday services. Not only do I proclaim the Good News in the pulpit, but at rest homes, at 10-year-olds' T-ball games, at hospitals, at gravesides, at weddings, and at fellowship meals. Evidently a part of anointing is who the preacher is and what people believe about him. So anointing for me is a matter of availability to God and a heart for God. My conclusion is that as I am willing to proclaim the Good News as needed and directed by the Lord, He, in turn, anoints me as His servant in the interruptions and in the pulpit.

His summary deserves meticulous attention by all who do ministry: "God is always faithful to compensate and empower my work via His anointing when I allow Him to set my agenda for ministry. When He determines the priorities, I need not be afraid of being taken away from one task to do another."

## Anointing Comes as Personal Weakness

Pastor Larry Rapp is an example of a nontraditional new breed of pastors who have entered contemporary ministry as a second career. Larry entered ministry after years as a cabinetmaker. He is married to Lola, an ordained minister who shares his pastoral work.

In a personal letter, after making a strong case for thorough preparation as part of his preaching manuscripted sermons, Rapp observed, "For me unction has little to do with thorough intellectual preparation. Fully prepared, I have gone into the pulpit feeling the desperate need to have the Lord do something beyond myself but through me. I often feel what I have to offer is too weak, even though I am carefully prepared. I sometimes actually tell Lola, 'I don't think it is good enough.'" Again, we face that recurring theme from several preachers of doing one's best but knowing it is not enough.

Larry continues with this distinctive concept:

Sometimes the unction came when I actually woke up Sunday morning prepared but feeling ill. Sometimes I was actually ill, and sometimes I felt under an attack that resulted in physical symptoms. Though I am not given to overly spiritualizing these kinds of things, I have come to believe these physical problems are attacks from the enemy of God and His Church. So in the hard times, I am learning to relax and even anticipate because I know these attacks often mean I have something significant to say, and I can expect anointing on the sermon. So for me, the unction of God most often comes in the midst of my feeling inadequate or even physical weakness.

Then Pastor Rapp adds, "To receive anointing mandates that it be preceded by prayer and fasting, and the sermon is delivered as a soul burden to people we love. So often, anointing for the people of God means they sense hearing another Voice. I've noticed under the anointing that a direct, hard-hitting, confrontational sermon often comes out in love more than in 'pet peeving.' Maybe that's because it is more God's message than mine."

### Anointing—When Everything Comes Together

Every pastor has high esteem for an elder ministerial statesman who has impacted his or her growth and development. For me, such a sturdy stalwart is John E. Riley, now retired. He was formerly a pastor and the president of Northwest Nazarene College in Nampa, Idaho. Though in his 80s, Dr. John and his wife, Dorcas, continued to lend spiritual strength and loving support to many worthy projects. Recently I was moved Godward when I heard him read scripture and pray in a worship service in an academic seminar.

After observing in a letter that a preacher's public utterance should flow from a background of lifelong honest preparation and holy living, Riley observed, "There are occasions—would God they might come more frequently—when everything seems to come together, and the Lord breathes upon and into and through the preacher in a blessed way that we call 'unction.' It is something like the healing of the woman with an issue of blood; Jesus said, 'Virtue is gone out from me,' and the woman was healed."

Riley continues with stimulating discernment:

How can I describe anointing? On those inspired occasions, one feels that to be spokesman for the Lord is the greatest privilege in the world. It includes having a sermon that seems the right word for the time; a congregation that seems open to and longing for truth; a mind that is totally alert; a voice that seems trumpetlike; words, ideas, concepts, illustrations that seem alive and dynamic; emotions, powerful yet controlled in the preacher, shared like electricity by the people. And in it all, God, the preacher, and the people seem to be interconnected as to be one.

Dr. Riley adds, "It is often like a sudden effusion, with the presence and power of Jesus. When the preacher is thus anointed and the people are blessed, it is so warm and bright that no one wants to leave. But when they do, they say, 'God was with us this morning. The Lord spoke to us today,' even though they know the preacher delivered the message."

Then with a look backward across a lifetime of fulfilling Christian service, Riley concludes: "As I look back across the years, how I wish the Lord had used me more effectively. And now I sit, in the pew most of the time, and I pray for the preacher, 'Dear Lord, anoint him so that others may be blessed.'"

## TRY APPLYING BIBLICAL PREACHING THEMES TO YOUR SERMONS

Wherever you may be reading this book, I suspect you are getting ready to preach again or have just finished preaching. Or to put it another way, every preacher will soon preach again, hopefully better the next time. Since we are in this task together—or should I say we are all alone?—I suggest you choose at least one biblical declaration about preaching as your own. I take comfort and strength for my preaching tasks from the apostle John's accurate assurance, "You have an anointing from the Holy One, and all of you know the truth" (1 John 2:20).

Preaching is God's idea, and He has set us apart to do it effectively for Him. To help refocus your preaching, try taking one of the following biblical examples of anointing to your congregation. You will likely increase your own anointing quotient in the process.

*"He has anointed me to preach."*

What would happen if a preacher took the words of our Lord "He has anointed me to preach" as his own and paid any price to be able to say, "The Spirit of the Lord is on me, because he has anointed me to preach" (Luke 4:18*a*)?

If that isn't enough to challenge every sermon and stimulate your prayers, then follow Jesus further in your own proclamation efforts "to preach good news to the poor." Follow that with a straightforward effort to "proclaim freedom for the prisoners and recovery of sight for the blind" (v. 18*b*).

*"Repent and be baptized, every one of you."*

Again, every contemporary preacher might spiritually impact the parish, community, denomination, or world by taking to his or her own hearers the announcement Peter made to an unfriendly crowd (Acts 2:14 ff.). Peter reminded them, "These men are not drunk, as you suppose. It's only nine in the morning!" (v. 15). Or from every sacred desk, let us preach Peter's emphatic conclusion, "Repent and be baptized, every one of you, in the name of Jesus Christ for the forgiveness of your sins" (v. 38). That's an eternally contemporary message that will fire the preacher and convict hearers of their need of God.

*"We cannot help speaking what we have seen and heard."*

Peter, the formerly frightened and sometimes distant follower of Jesus, experienced a transformation of character and found a new surge of courage when he preached twice following the cripple's healing at the Temple gate. Remember the passage? The priests, the captains of the Temple guard, and the Sadducees commanded Peter and John not to speak in Jesus' name. In response, Peter answered with an incredible anointing, "Whether it be right in the sight of God to hearken unto you more than unto God, judge ye. For we cannot but speak the things which we have seen and heard" (Acts 4:19-20, KJV). What powerful words of personal faith, and what a steadfast resolution for empowered preaching!

The Early Church then had a prayer meeting, and the record says, "They spake the word of God with boldness" (v.

31, KJV). Peter and John experienced supernatural unction for speaking a word that made a magnificent difference. They shared the Good News that was personal, life-changing, and buoyant to the Early Church. The Word changed them, changed the Church, and impacted people around them who were not a part of their fellowship.

*"My preaching [was] with a demonstration of the Spirit's power."*

What would happen to the people we serve if we made Paul's experience our own? His words are spiritual dynamite for every age: "When I came to you, brothers, I did not come with eloquence or superior wisdom as I proclaimed to you the testimony about God. For I resolved to know nothing while I was with you except Jesus Christ and him crucified. I came to you in weakness and fear, and with much trembling. My message and my preaching were not with wise and persuasive words, but with a demonstration of the Spirit's power, so that your faith might not rest on men's wisdom, but on God's power" (1 Cor. 2:1-5).

Take those sentences apart, consider them carefully, exegete them meticulously. Then apply these realities to so many contemporary pulpits, maybe yours, where eloquence, superior wisdom, and persuasive words are frequently considered more valuable than the Spirit's demonstration and power. No eloquence, no superior wisdom, no tricky information—just the demonstration and power of the Holy Spirit. And that's more than enough.

*"We preach . . . Christ the power of God and the wisdom of God."*

Another probing refocus on preaching comes from another of Paul's strong statements: "God was pleased through the foolishness of what was preached to save those who believe. Jews demand miraculous signs and Greeks look for wisdom, but we preach Christ crucified. . . . Christ the power of God and the wisdom of God" (1 Cor. 1:21-24). I have a treasured friend who, when he was elected to the highest office in his denomination, received letters from hundreds of common people urging him to preach Christ. That's what people want to hear. That's what people need. That's what will renew the Church in every generation. And that's what will keep you preaching through thick and thin for a lifetime.

*"Woe to me if I do not preach the gospel."*

Other examples from the apostle Paul might be used: "By the power of the Spirit of God . . . I have fully preached the gospel" (Rom. 15:19, KJV); "Christ sent me . . . to preach the gospel" (1 Cor. 1:17, KJV); "Woe is unto me, if I preach not the gospel!" (9:16, KJV).

A similar exercise, though tailor-made by you, can be taken from a variety of other biblical passages in both Old and New Testaments.

## THE HOLY AUDACITY OF ANOINTING

Some things, such as God creating the world and creating my family and friends, are not hard for me to imagine. It does not seem too mind-boggling for me to accept God as being in charge of the whole human race, though I wonder if that must not sometimes give Him nightmares. And it is easy to comprehend that He knows more than anyone else.

But it's almost too much for me when I picture God coming into my musty basement study to inspire my getting ready to preach next Sunday to people who sometimes seem bored with my preaching. Could it be that God visits me in that place where I study, with its secondhand desk, Kmart drapes, old folding chair, dusty bookcases, and 10-year-old, slow-response computer? It tests plausibility even more for me to think that the God of heaven speaks through my stammering tongue, my hardheadedness, my closed-mindedness, and my limited experience as I hold His Best-seller in my hands. I know I cannot do it well enough for Him. His people deserve more than I am able to give them. And yet He puts His reputation on the line when He uses the likes of me.

# 5

# Supernatural Muscle in Christ's Service

## Divine Enablement Produces Lasting Achievement

"What kind of power does the big guy mean?" an eight-year-old girl asked her parents following my sermon. Evidently her class at school had been studying a unit on electricity and wind power.

Her question, however, stands at the center of contemporary life. Power apparently attracts and repels almost everyone. Even when we try to forget power, control, and authority for an hour or two, some report of abuse of civic or church power appears on the evening news. Face it—power and money run society, and this sinister force shows up in the Church more than we want to admit.

No price seems too high for the pyramiding of power for too many who claim to be followers of the powerless Jesus. The size of the prize doesn't seem to matter much. Those with power, those who want power, and those with no power—all seem eager to gain more control. One little boy explained our dilemma: "My grandma bosses my mom, my mom bosses my dad, my dad bosses me, I boss the dog, and he barks at the neighbors." How true! And to complicate matters even more, new power groups keep springing up in our society demanding Black power, female power, Hispanic power, youth power, gray power, and homosexual power.

After Watergate and a prison term, Charles Colson

warned, "The quest for power is like the dryness of a man drinking salt water. The more he drinks, the more he demands. His thirst is never quenched." Then he continues, "It was in prison that I discovered that the only way to satisfy the thirst for power is through the Living Water."[1] Paul the apostle agrees that the driving force for all Kingdom achievement must be God himself rather than our own power needs when he wrote, "We pray that you'll have the strength to stick it out over the long haul—not the grim strength of gritting your teeth but the glory-strength God gives. It is strength that endures the unendurable and spills over into joy, thanking the Father who makes us strong enough to take part in everything bright and beautiful that he has for us" (Col. 1:11-12, TM).

## TWO SIGNIFICANTLY DIFFERENT KINDS OF POWER

History shows that the Church has struggled for almost 2,000 years to reconcile two radically different kinds of power. The confusion continues, even though Jesus showed us how to sort through the differences two millennia ago. The two competing, confusing powers are (1) controlling ecclesiastical authority over some part of the Church and (2) a supernatural energizing by the Spirit of God to help ordinary people achieve extraordinary accomplishments to do Christ's work in the world.

The resulting dead-end conflict is accurately stated in these insightful sentences from writer Gayle D. Erwin: "Christ Jesus made himself nothing. He made himself nothing, emptied himself—the great *kenosis*. He made himself of no reputation, no image. . . . But reputation is so important to me. I want to be seen with the right people, remembered in the right light, advertised with my name spelled right, live in the right neighborhood, drive the right kind of car, wear the right kind of clothing. But Jesus made himself of no reputation."[2]

Consider the Father's scale of values. God puts enablement power high on His agenda. It is so important in His priorities that Scripture takes 28 chapters in the Book of Acts to show how this divine enduement flows through Christ-centered believers to spiritually transform the world. That is why Acts is among the most spiritually electrifying literature ever written.

This supernatural power found in Scripture equips believers to impact their world for Christ. This empowerment enables believers in every new generation to accomplish extraordinary exploits for the Kingdom. Endued people, accomplishing supernatural achievements for Christ, can be met all along the front lines of Christian history. The purpose of this supernatural kind of power is to help believers fully enjoy Christ-saturated lives, a quality of life that makes it possible to live the way God intended when He created us. Though it may not always be high voltage, it is the inner strength to live a Christlike life. J. I. Packer says this power "calls our attention to God omnipotently at work before our eyes, with a purpose of involving us in what He is doing."[3]

God's holy enablement, a life-giving spring, flows through a pure heart. Some people mistakenly seek the power without purity. This holy life produces a single-minded devotion to what God wants. Its fruits are supernatural stamina, rugged tenacity, scrubbed-clean motivation, disarming tenderness, animated passion for an eternal cause, a quiet force for righteousness, and greatness in residence. It motivates serious disciples to make imaginative innovation in ministry strategies. A spiritually empowered believer sometimes experiences all of these, sometimes one of them, and sometimes much more. The bottom line of enablement—a thoroughly dedicated human being linked to the empowerment of God—can accomplish amazing Kingdom achievements.

This "strong weakness" is more than professional, cultural, or educational strengths, though it augments and enhances them. From a purely human perspective, God's plan to infuse empowerment into our yielded human frailty seems impossible or even ridiculous. But His strategies often surprise us.

This vitality from beyond makes it possible for believers to triumph in whatever life brings. This enablement from the Holy One flows into the details of a human life and is God's response to William Law's description of human weakness: "For we cannot lift up a hand, or stir our food, but by a power that is lent us from God."[4]

In God's system of values, unlimited commitment is significantly more important than bulging muscles or razor-sharp minds. In one succinct sentence, Paul summarizes the mind of God regarding this enablement: "For Christ's sake, I delight in weaknesses, in insults, in hardships, in persecutions, in difficulties. For when I am weak, then I am strong" (2 Cor. 12:10). This means God supplies enablement for me to do every good work.

The possibilities are miraculous and marvelous. God makes the impossible possible. He beefs up human effort with supernatural power. This enablement, however, never gets set in motion until a believer starts by giving his or her human best. Here's the process: First a believer commits soul and will, and then brain and brawn can be empowered by God. Songwriter Annie Johnson Flint described this dynamic process well: "When we reach the end of our hoarded resources, / Our Father's full giving is only begun."* Thoroughly yielded servants need God to do so much more through them than they can do by themselves. And He does.

Then their listeners are moved to supernatural action by their enabled sermons.

Then their anointed teaching becomes refreshing water in the desert to those who are touched by their ministry.

Then the crust of bread they offer a hungry soul becomes better than prime rib.

Then the believer writes an ordinary letter or shares a greeting that changes a life.

Then the empowered one shares a life-sustaining word of affirmation that lifts a drooping spirit.

All this transpires as the believer trusts God with his or her wholly yielded, feeble efforts that the Father uses to revolutionize people, churches, and communities. This is an adventuresome connection with Omnipotence.

## THIS HOLY ENERGY PRODUCES MIRACULOUS RESULTS

Dip into the New Testament almost anywhere, especially in Acts, to see for yourself how this enabling works. It is an impressive record of how holy enablement energized adventuresome living, healed brokenness, and completed incompleteness.

This supernatural power, like a valuable diamond, has many enchanting facets. British journalist Malcolm Muggeridge, who came to faith late in his life after interviewing Mother Teresa, describes divine power as "muscle in the service of Christ." Muggeridge saw it in abundant supply in the little Calcutta nun who has impacted the whole world with her service and witness.

Last Sunday our pastor called this enablement "a holy energy for achieving what God wants us to do." Best-seller author Stephen R. Covey offers us a definitive description of power as "the faculty or capacity to act, the strength and potency to accomplish something. It is the vitality to make choices and decisions. It also includes the capacity to overcome deeply embedded habits and to cultivate higher, more effective ones."[5] Covey's summation squares with what God promises in Scripture and delivers in life.

Bible scholar William Barclay describes the results of this empowered life: "When the Spirit of God enters a man, his weakness is clad with the power of God. He is enabled to do the undoable, and to face the unfaceable, and to bear the unbearable."[6] This empowerment is the way God strides into the details of our living. The apostle Paul reminds us of Christ's comforting words: "It is in weakness that my power becomes more powerful" (2 Cor. 12:9, BARCLAY).

## THIS ENABLEMENT WORKS IN ORDINARY PEOPLE

For us to fully understand and receive this enablement, several compelling questions need to be asked and answered: Does this enablement make a significant difference in daily events? If yes, how? Is it reserved for supersaints? Can common people have it on bad days? And can it work in secular dimensions of life? The answer to all these queries is a resounding *yes!*

First-century disciples experienced supernatural equipping as their earthly association with Jesus came to an end. It took place within them at a turbulent time when God commissioned them with the weighty responsibility to continue "all that Jesus began to do and to teach" (Acts 1:1). What a charge, and what a challenge. And for its accomplishment, Jesus promised that the Holy Spirit "lives with you and will be in you" (John 14:17).

The original disciples couldn't help but wonder: Does Jesus know how many times we have failed? Does He know our weaknesses? How can we do it? What does Jesus want done? How can we measure up to such an unbelievable challenge? They questioned how such weaklings could achieve such accomplishments for Him.

Their confusion and spiritual inferiority complexes changed as divine enablement began working through them. They became flesh-and-blood examples of the supernatural power and promise of Jesus. Their weak dependency was the starting point for the achievement God would do through them, as it has always been since New Testament times.

Consider how the disciples were affected. These early Christian leaders found it difficult to think clearly following the Crucifixion because of their hang-ups about power. They expected prominence but experienced obscurity. And in spite of grandiose notions about being rulers and kings, they hobbled into a coldhearted world; they were penniless, ignored, and without a shred of social standing. They wanted royalty but received privation. Their situation seemed bleak and hopeless. It was. It was so disheartening that the pessimists of their group were quick to predict even more failures ahead.

Their bewilderment multiplied still more as Jesus commanded, "You will be witnesses for Me in the whole world." His words intensified the perplexities beyond anything they could imagine. The implications of His instructions baffled them as much as their frailties frightened them. So much about the Kingdom disappointed and confused them.

Their fears and frustrations went off the Richter scale

when Jesus explained the part He wanted them to accomplish in world evangelization. Their first assignment was their hometown, "Jerusalem"—a place of slow beginnings, embarrassing past failures, and incredible risks. Then to "Judea and Samaria," including frightening foreign frontiers with strange geography, cultures, and racial notions. The next part of the commission was still more demanding—to go "to the ends of the earth" (Acts 1:8). Such a mind-staggering global expansion went beyond anything they ever imagined for themselves or anyone else.

God's picture was too big for them, just as it so often is for us. His plans frequently seem too difficult for even His most committed servants. Knowing all of this made the disciples think like Pogo, "We are confronted with insurmountable opportunities." Their assignment terrorized them just as ours sometimes panics us.

In the midst of this chilling fear, the disciples learned a lesson that has shaped all the intervening history of the Christian Church: God never assigns His followers anything without supplying enablement. Without fail, His mandates are always fully supported by supernatural enablement. Oswald Chambers clarifies this issue: "The thing that taxes almightiness is the very thing which we as disciples of Jesus ought to believe He will do. We impoverish His ministry the moment we forget He is Almighty; the impoverishment is in us, not in Him. We will come to Jesus as Comforter or as Sympathizer, but we will not come to Him as Almighty."[7]

As those folks who experienced the Upper Room followed Christ with radical obedience, supernatural assistance tore down the stumbling blocks. Fear turned to courage. Weakness was transformed into strength. Shyness became boldness. Doubt was transformed into faith. The Father demonstrated to them His wide-opened secret: God empowers ordinary people to change His world.

One fact is clear, now and then: God works through people who know they cannot do much without Him. Supernatural enablement is the way weak, wavering, problem-oriented disciples in every generation became sturdy Kingdom achievers. They accomplished amazing victories. They added thousands to their fellowship. They experienced incredible achievements for God's kingdom and delightful spiritual growth for themselves.

### THE BETHLEHEM BABY MODELS "STRONG WEAKNESS"

At the first Christmas, God modeled how this mighty weakness works. Into a world helplessly oppressed by Roman authority and mesmerized by Jewish regulations, the Father surprised humankind by sending His Son as a manger babe to penniless, powerless, unsophisticated, young parents. God overcame the world at Bethlehem by apparently being overcome. What took place there in the straw offers us an astonishing example of how God uses weak, insignificant things to confound the mighty.

God used the utter dependence of the infant Jesus to dethrone Roman splendor and Jewish tradition. At Bethlehem He showed the world the weakness of secular and ecclesiastical power. This defenseless Baby who owned nothing became the Savior who gave us everything that matters. This powerhouse of weakness—the Christ child—forever shattered our concepts concerning military might, the control of religious leaders, and our own watertight systems of logic. No one fully understands how weakness becomes strength in God's way of doing things. But it does. And the God of the universe shows His evidence in a humble virgin girl, her carpenter husband, and her helpless Baby.

Jesus fully explained this concept in the vine passage: "You can do nothing without Me, but with Me you can do everything I want done" (see John 15:5). Evangelist Howard O. Jones condensed this teaching into a pithy sentence: "I can do only as I depend."[8]

### NO SELF-SOVEREIGNTY ALLOWED

God requires, however, that one significant condition of this supernatural power must be met. Dependence must be acknowledged before one can receive divine enablement. Our Lord has no patience with our swaggering self-sovereignty or our silly pride for ability that He gave us. The condition of receiving His power is voluntary relinquishment of all control of our lives to Him.

A Christ-saturated corporation president kept the control issue in perspective with a wall plaque in his office: "In this place there is to be full recognition of the superior power of Jesus Christ." Even though we humanly hesitate admitting dependence, we know we are not able to do much without this superior power of Jesus Christ. And who would attempt to run his or her own show when the benefits are fully understood?

## How the Enablement Process Works

How does God's enablement work in my life and ministry?

The starting gate requires a disciple to do his or her best, seeking to be as competent as possible; then God adds the rest. I admit to being baffled by what a regular Joe or an ordinary Jane can be and do with God's help. But after we do our best and turn to Him the rest, He enables service that we could never accomplish with our own tenacity, strength, or intelligence. Holy enablement comes when we admit our full dependence on Him and abandon our hunger for dominance. Oswald Chambers advises the authentic disciple of Christ:

> The reason some of us are such poor specimens of Christianity is because we have no Almighty Christ. We have Christian attributes and experiences, but there is no abandonment to Jesus Christ. When we get into difficult circumstances, we impoverish His ministry by saying—"Of course He cannot do anything," and we struggle down to the deeps and try to get the water for ourselves. Beware of the satisfaction of sinking back and saying—"It can't be done"; you know it can be done if you look to Jesus. The well of your incompleteness is deep, but make the effort and look away to Him.[9]

That means God's enablement comes only when I pray with childlike dependence, "I've done my best, and I need You to do the rest." The divine empowerment, God's "something more," is activated when our best effort is coupled with wholehearted reliance on Him.

God's surprising lessons in human powerlessness and supernatural enablement are never learned by those who watch from the bleachers. Nor can they be learned by those who think they know everything or can do anything; the Holy Spirit usually allows the know-alls and be-alls to embarrass themselves in their own failures. However, His empowerment is always available to dependent disciples who minister at the cutting edge of Kingdom interests.

When human commitment, understanding, and abilities get pushed to the limit, it is obvious that our grit is not enough. We learn what God can do through us when we go out on the limb, where smug strength and prideful intelligence will not support us—but He does.

## Old Testament Examples

The Old Testament records many examples of God's response to human powerlessness. The pattern is clear: Do all you can. Trust all you can. And then marvel at what God does.

Jordan's soggy riverbed miraculously became a dry footpath when the priests' feet touched the water's edge. Neither the human action nor the supernatural outcome fit any human logic, experience, or ability.

Fiery furnace deliverance, never available to mere bystanders, came to those who trusted God with radical obedience and courageous witness. God provided exactly what the obedient Hebrew brothers needed in the nick of time, and that was soon enough.

Armchair theorists could not take one shred of credit for even a tiny crack in the walls of Jericho. God used the marchers one step at a time as they followed His direction. As a result, those marching participants had full confidence that the wall would tumble down, and it did.

## New Testament Pattern

Holy achievement, near the dawn of Christian history, had nothing to do with organizational status but everything to do with divine assistance. The first-generation disciples revolutionized their world because they were energized by the Holy Spirit, so they had Christlike love, invincible faith, and supernatural stamina. It started inside them because they enjoyed a supernatural connection with Omnipotence, and they knew it.

## Jesus Required a Holy Wait

For a variety of reasons, scholars often suggest the Book of Acts might be more accurately named "The Acts of the Holy Spirit." But "A Record of How the Holy Spirit Empowers Average Folks" might be even more true to the facts.

The disciples' successes started with a long, well-focused wait. By human logic, our Lord's mandate to wait seemed like an irrational way to mobilize a moral and spiritual reformation. But even though some participants probably murmured about what they thought was such an absurd idea, they waited as Jesus commanded them. Of course, God did not need their waiting, but they did. Their 10-day wait gave them a new understanding of their task and helped them see their own needs before they were able to demonstrate maximum usefulness for God.

As they waited, surprising spin-offs happened. They were empowered for their immediate task in the Upper Room. Remarkable bonds of strengthening relationships developed between them as they prayed (1:14). They enjoyed fellowship (v. 14), gained new insight from Scripture (v. 16), and chose future leaders. The connections they developed with God and each other during their wait prepared them for their future frontline efforts for the gospel.

In the Upper Room frightened cowards were miraculously transformed into outspoken achievers. The inactive among them were kindled with soul passion for an eternal cause. They became exuberantly effective. Silent members started speaking life-giving words. And God transformed doubters into doers.

None of them could have predicted they could do so much for the Kingdom. They surprised themselves and each other. They had no idea what God would do through them.

They did not realize where this supernatural muscle in service for Christ would take them. They marveled that supernatural achievement seemed built into all their future.

One Sabbath near the beginning of their ministry together, this awe-inspiring energy in the work of God caused a rowdy commotion on the porch of the Temple. Then the ordinary quickly became the extraordinary. The crowd, as well as the disciples, were dumbfounded by the spectacle of a healed cripple jumping about praising God (Acts 3:9-19). Some speculated. Some scorned. Some rejoiced. Like a swelling ocean current, amazement rippled through the crowd to the top religious and civic authorities. And those religious leaders began worrying immediately about losing control.

As a result, the disciples were summoned to appear before the big guns of authority—rulers and teachers of the law—who thoroughly interrogated them about their procedures and authority. The leaders could not believe that the uneducated disciples could heal a lame man and create such an uproar. They asked the official question, "By what power or what name did you do this?" (4:7). The answer was simple, focused, and supernatural. They did it in the power of God, and the name of Jesus was their authority.

**Empowerment for Contemporary Christian Service**

This record teaches several timeless lessons for disciples in every generation. This supernatural muscle in service for Christ takes disciples where they could never go without divine aid or where they could never function without Him. A comparable daring and a comparable achievement are needed now more than ever.

Here's an interesting question well worth our consideration: If we waited in our own upper rooms, might today's Church enjoy similar results? Might it be that we could be energized by the prayer Albert Day described as "the passionate fervor of a whole self that pants to know God and His will above all knowing"?[10]

Then again, purposeful waiting today might help the contemporary Church become stirred by Scripture so it has a powerful new Bible in which the Spirit interprets the Resurrection, illumines the miracles, revitalizes relationships with Christ, prepares disciples for His return, and helps us more fully understand our contemporary settings for ministry. Such waiting might defrost the Church's stagnation into an obedient fellowship determined to please Christ alone.

The Church in every age must be empowered if it is to have either quality or quantity growth. Both are needed. The Father intends for each new generation to win their world through enabled believers. His plan is still in place. He wants the Church to revolutionarily impact the culture for Christ. And He wants to use ordinary, common, enabled people like us to do it.

As a new century commences, the contemporary Church is greatly confused about power. In our time in church history, divine enablement for noteworthy achievement is virtually ignored. We have learned to depend, to our peril, on ourselves—our education, money, strategy, personnel, facilities, and experience. But it is obvious we need more power.

At the same time, abused and misused organizational authority and ecclesiastical control are tolerated, sometimes encouraged, and often paralyzing to the cause. The result is little or no achievement of Kingdom objectives. The contemporary Church is stalled by its own bloated bureaucracy and often wastes its energy rearranging the deck chairs on a sinking ship.

Today's Church is in peril because many good talkers parade throughout her ranks as creative achievers. Image and impression are confused with substance and strength. Being "a good ol' team player" is confused with supernaturally fueled achievement. Many counterfeit pacesetters, without doing much for the Kingdom, succeed in building false reputations for themselves. Often they are given significant leadership assignments but hinder the Church and allow her to settle for no achievement. It happens on all levels of church life.

I heard recently about a little grandmother who controls a church of 50 people with her money and her ability to play the piano; for 30 years she has ruled or ruined. The lamenta-

ble results, of course, are unwon converts, undernourished
believers, lethargic churches, and verbose self-promoters who
pretend to be leaders. In secular vocations such practices
would be considered malfeasance of duty. As a result of this
hindrance, the Church in two or three more generations is
likely to have little spiritual muscle and no heavenly vision.

Let's squarely face our contemporary situation. More ac-
tivism will not alleviate our predicament. But Francis Schaeffer offers a miracle remedy: "Doing the Lord's work in the
Lord's way is not some exotic thing; rather it is having and
practicing the mentality which Christ commands."[11]

### Empowerment Fueled Church Growth

The first disciples achieved abundant accomplishments
that changed their world. The Church grew because of the
converts they won. Though they probably never intended to
receive personal satisfaction, it spread like heavenly manna
all around them as they declared their Christ-centered message with holy recklessness. They were neither bored nor
burned out. They were willing to die for the cause of Christ
and counted such a possibility a privilege. Similar achievements could happen again if we want them.

The Early Church found God's ways stimulating, invigo-
rating, and productive. Pentecost changed them so that they
did a complete turnaround. They were delivered from their
locked-door mentality at the last meal or their mass defection
at the time of our Lord's arrest. The contrast between their
lives after Pentecost and Peter's denial, or their dreary melan-
choly near the end of Holy Week, is absolutely amazing.

Now as always, growing churches require bold action
like what the Early Church experienced after Pentecost. Our
strategies, like theirs, must be empowered and directed by
the Spirit of God. The way to victorious achievement in our
time is not to try to go back to the Early Church or back to
Luther or Wesley, but to take the energizing Spirit they had
into the depths of our own characters and to the front lines of
contemporary despair and moral confusion. Then the God of
the Early Church, the God of Luther, and the God of Wesley

will apply the gospel to our time just as He did to theirs.

It's time to pray with former Methodist bishop Ralph Cushman:

> *Renew their breed, Almighty God!*
> *Those pioneers of yesterday . . .*
> *New frontiers lift their rocky heights,*
> *New deserts stretch before our years;*
> *Renew in us, Almighty God,*
> *The spirit of the pioneers.*[12]

The question awaits our commitment: Will we intentionally renew the supernatural power of God in the 21st-century Church?

# 6

# Power—Gluttony That Sabotages Ministry

## Authority Abusers Gridlock the Church

A power monster is choking contemporary Christianity to death. Abused authority is among the Church's most frustrating roadblocks and her most unspoken agony. When human control of the Church supplants Christlike love, the achievement of her New Testament mission slows to a snail's pace. The outcome is a frustrating distortion of what God intends ministry to be. This problem reaches from the Vatican to the rural crossroads church where Aunt Sally always gets her way. Offenders can be found standing in pulpits and sitting in pews.

Laughably but tragically, many ploys for gaining power are mistakenly called "ministry." In the confusion, relationships originally built on biblical teaching and vigorous faith have soured into a struggle over who controls the church. To put the problem in proper perspective, the existing situation must be judged against the way Jesus handled power. He used a manger, mud from spittle, a towel, a bit of grain, a cross, a borrowed tomb, and Easter morning. In contrast, modern power brokers use flattery, maneuvering, doublespeak, money, and lobbying.

Destructive use of power doggedly pursues position, prominence, pride, and control. Kingdom use of power gives itself to service, sacrifice, surrender, and selflessness that produces incredible satisfaction and amazing results. The first use of power intoxicates with self-importance; the second inspires devotion. One wants to be first; the other, last. The first disappoints; the second satisfies. One bores, but the other gets better with use. One inflates unrealistic expectations, while the other promises lasting rewards. The controlling kind of power puffs up, whereas the other produces humility.

Power gluttony grows like a flesh-eating infection in the inner part of a human being. It infects the soul whenever clergy or lay leaders try to pyramid legitimate authority into domination. It can happen at every level of the Church's life—local congregations, parachurch organizations, independent churches, and denominations. Dag Hammarskjöld describes how it often starts: "Around a man who has been pushed into the limelight, a legend begins to grow as it does around a dead man. But a dead man is in no danger of yielding to the temptation to nourish his legend, or accept its picture as reality. I pity the man who falls in love with his image as it is drawn by public opinion during the honeymoon of publicity."[1]

The power czar's ugly, fragmented inner world is bluntly pictured by R. Paul Stevens in *Liberating the Laity:* "While we say Christ is the King of the church, we treat Him like the Queen of England, as a figurehead, a constitutional monarch who reigns but does not rule. Church leaders assume the throne while claiming they honor the reign of the King himself."[2] This alluring self-delusion makes a leader usurp privileges that belong only to God.

Greed for power creates destructive consequences in church life and in the end condemns those who seek it. Power misuse always puts a lid of mediocrity on ministry. Like poison dripping into a person's veins, power abuse cripples the leader spiritually and, if not stopped, ultimately destroys the congregation, the organization, and the abuser's soul. Selfish motives for leading always create some kind of leadership crisis or work stoppage. Let's get brutally honest. Something is desperately out of sync in the Body of Christ when a highly visible church leader tells a young pastor, "I hate the travel but love the power." For that leader, power had become an end (self-promotion) and not a means for accomplishing ministry. The Church has serious problems when grasping for power supplants selfless service, so "Christian leaders draw farther and farther away from mutuality, intimacy and accountability to the body of Christ."[3]

To escape these hazardous gridlocks, scrupulous Christian leaders must examine their use of and desire for power. To define the scope of this discussion, by "leaders" we mean every committee member, pastor, lay leader, church administrator, Christian educator, parachurch officer, or anyone else who influences the church in any way, small or great.

## KEY FACTS ABOUT THE USE OF AUTHORITY

Organizational authority, though it is morally neutral in itself, is a necessary ingredient for achievement. Nothing happens in any group until someone leads, decides, motivates, or uses authority properly. Unused authority never accomplishes anything, and nonuse of power can be as harmful as misuse; to be able to do something but refuse to do it may be among the worst of all transgressions against God. Thus it may be helpful to consider the following principles.

• **Everyone controls someone or something.** Everyone has some control over family, job, or neighborhood. Newborns have power to keep their parents awake all night. Aged parents control their families, even though they live miles apart. Everyone possesses some power, though everyone may not realize it or know how to use it.

This fact raises these questions: How do I treat subordinates? How do I use my power? How do I respond to power abusers? Even apparently powerless people must weigh how they use their control over others.

• **All authority is temporary.** Its fleeting nature shows when a person of position retires, dies, or changes assignments. Then, in a surprisingly short time, power passes to others. In the natural scheme of things, no one keeps control of Kingdom efforts for more than a few years.

• **Authority has many roots.** Hendrick Smith lists the roots of power that go beyond obvious sources like position, status, and organizational control when he says, "Information and knowledge are power. Visibility is power. A sense of timing is power. Trust and integrity are power. Personal energy is power and so is self-confidence. Showmanship is power. Likability is power. Access to the inner sanctum is power. Obstruction and delay are power. Winning is power. The illusion of authority is even sometimes power."[4] But there is more—in Christian organizations, the ultimate and most authentic source of authority comes from geniune godliness and selfless efforts for Christ.

• **Authority abuse always starts small.** Authority abuse usually commences with almost imperceptible microsteps. The downward spiral often starts with an area of strength like public speaking, gifted writing, intellectual prowess, or moneymaking ability. Wesley Pippert calls this downward progression "microscopic misdemeanors" that at first seem minor, like "a bit too much pride here, a bit of an inclination to cut corners, to take advantage of others, and a desire to cling to power at all costs."[5] An auditor in the business world might call these first steps "petty larceny." Abuse frequently starts in tiny untruths we want to believe about ourselves and with petty falsehoods we want others to believe about us.

• **Power greed has little to do with the size of the prize.** Power can be enticingly seductive even when dealing with insignificant projects in tiny groups. Like ducks fighting for a bread morsel on a pond or sandpipers vying for insects at the beach, individuals jockey to get a job that controls 2 people or jostle to boss a 25-member church. Even for the smallest stakes, power sometimes tempts a janitor or a bishop, an usher or the pope, a Sunday School teacher or a church treasurer.

• **Power never produces achievement until it is shared.** Members of groups are energized for magnificent attainment when a leader trusts them. Effectiveness for Christian causes often begins when the highest authority figure recognizes others as being capable, trustworthy, and committed to the cause. Then everyone benefits because followers feel empowered to work at maximum efficiency with permission to use their creative imagination.

## POWER ADDICTS WANT MORE

Love of titles, expected entitlement, exploitive relationships, and seeking a seat at the head table are symptoms of ecclesiastical power addictions. In many congregations and organizations, these detrimental symptoms eat away at the leader's inner life like a cancer, and yet they are often accepted as the norm. Management specialist Peter Drucker sounds like the apostle Paul when he warns, "Rank does not corner privilege or give power. It imposes responsibility."[6] Greed for power, even when it comes dressed in Sunday church clothes, is only a well-dressed rascal.

Power-grasping symptoms often begin as quiet "me-first-ism." President John R. O'Neil of the California School of Professional Psychology comments, "Unlike the real nourishment of doing and producing, status and power are like sugar or cocaine, leaving the consumer ever hungrier for more."[7] As a consequence, misused power keeps churches of all sizes from experiencing the energizing force of the gospel or the renewing impact of truth. This addictive power plague has several menacing symptoms:

1. A church leader assumes the position gives him or her superior intelligence or spirituality.

2. A church leader allows personal actions that invalidate the teachings of Jesus.

3. A church leader expects and accepts favored status.

4. A church leader forgets his or her accountability to God by making decisions to impress others.

5. A church leader thinks people are following when they are merely tolerating the leader.

6. A church leader holds power but refuses to use it.

7. A church leader is afraid to ask, "Is my leadership effort pleasing to Christ?"

God's verdict on misused power is tough. He abhors the haughty and the power seeker. He detests imitation piety. He refuses to keep company with those who practice expediency and moral shortcuts. But He offers something better that amazes modern manipulators. He surprises the secular power broker by empowering the weak, energizing the weary, speaking through stutterers, and revolutionizing a village, city, or nationality through some ordinary, obscure disciple of His.

## HOW ECCLESIASTICAL POWER ABUSERS BEHAVE

Though most power-hungry folks function differently in church than their counterparts in business or government, John W. Gardner's synopsis applies: "The truly modern dictator achieves his goals through the people, not in spite of them. He rides their aspirations to power. He manipulates their hopes and fears and is ushered into office with their joyous shouts."[8] This same thing happens in churches. Believers trust leaders whom they choose to lead. They reason that good people should not have to question the intentions or actions of a true spiritual leader. But it is almost impossible to forecast how any emerging leader will use authority or position, because power so easily seduces and so frequently corrupts. Even small amounts of authority change people, either for the better or worse; few stay the same.

### Self-deception

Power abusers can easily make themselves believe they are selfless. Those who observe wonder how they could make themselves believe such a whopper, as they manipulate perks, raises, and status for themselves at the expense of money, effort, and morale of the little people. However convincing this self-deception may seem to leaders, their power abuse still corrupts church groups, Sunday School classes, dioceses, presbyteries, judicatories, and denominations.

Power snatchers, when confronted with discrepancies between what they do and say, often appear to be momentarily chagrined, like children caught with their hands in cookie jars. But the pattern persists below the surface. For an illustration, consider several well-used strategies. Bogus pacesetters will only champion causes they get glory from leading. Or they deceive themselves into believing nepotism with their family members is good for the church. Or they fool themselves into believing they deserve favored status in budget expenditures. One church I know gave Mr. Key Layman a greatly increased insurance contract while refusing to give a youth pastor a modest and much-needed pay raise.

### Religious Double-talk

Church power graspers, while bashing secularists, frequently use religious language to camouflage their own similar aspirations. In a heart cluttered with power gluttony, manipulation gets easily confused with high-minded motivation. Then behind-the-scenes hardball politics is called "the will of God," while those who genuinely seek divine guidance shake their heads in amazement and confusion.

Like physical or emotional abusers, power abusers are generally respectable persons who function much of the time at normal standards of behavior. But churches often find themselves suffering at the hands of those who are selfless 95 percent of the time. The 5 percent is what undermines relationships, destroys confidence, and obstructs growth.

### Promote a Privileged Class

The Church does not exist to fulfill anyone's power needs, however piously they may be camouflaged. The Church exists to help people find salvation, grace, freedom, and healing for those times the world beats them and leaves them for dead. Those who lead are charged with expediting this process and not with promoting themselves or a select minority into a privileged class. Think how power abuse nauseates those who look on from the outside. And that may be the reason many alert insiders often lose interest and give up involvement.

### Hostage to Their Own Authority

Misused power fools leaders with a lethal illusion that they control power when, in truth, they are enslaved by it. Misused power corrupts the abusers' souls even as it makes them addicted to their own compulsions.

Like the skull and crossbones on a package of poison, controllers must be cautioned that power abuse shrivels the soul and at the same time jeopardizes the spiritual well-being of those who follow them. One preacher close to television evangelists' scandals confessed, "I was duped by my own lust for control. I called it 'ambition for God,' and my associates called it 'a selfish quest for power.'"

## Change in Unexpected Ways

In a congregation, national agency, or parachurch organization, abusers' obsessions do not generally appear until additional opportunities are given to control, or their authority is questioned. Then like an atomic bomb, something goes off that makes the abuser call attention to his or her rank or position. In such a mental state, the abuser may force personal opinions on subordinates, however ill advised. Such a person gets touchy over some imagined slight or insignificant event, becomes thoroughly absorbed with personal self-image, and distrusts followers' loyalty.

Abraham Lincoln was right: "Nearly all men can stand adversity, but if you want to test a man's character, give him power."[9] How true—a ravenous craving for power can transform congenial people into religious turncoats or holy terrors. The problem deepens even more when these inadequate warlords find it necessary to insulate themselves behind facades of artificial strength. This weakness expresses itself in demanding, authoritarian actions. Regrettably, these characteristics are easy to see in others and hard to see in ourselves. Without much effort, we can fool ourselves into believing long hours, lofty position, or even a span of control over others is the same as servanthood. But how does it look to Jesus?

## Do Little or Nothing

There is a strange contradiction that takes place when some power grabbers succeed in getting authority. Their idea is "I now have the prize—what do I do with it?" The very one who aspired to a position, after having gotten control, becomes unwilling to lead. It's something like a person buying a car who sits in it and admires the dashboard without starting the motor or taking a trip. Many who snatch the reins do not seem to know how to use them. Others are afraid to use them. So they do little or nothing but sound like a noisy gong that says over and over, "I am in charge."

## THE TRAUMA THAT POWER GRABBERS
## CAUSE IN CHURCHES

No vaccine has been discovered to inoculate persons against the power virus. Strangely, church organizations continue to shoot themselves in the feet by underplaying servanthood and deifying power—a blatant violation of God's command, "No other gods before me" (Exod. 20:3; Deut. 5:7). What does all this do to the churches and organizations?

### Misused Power Creates a Standstill Church

Some power tactics used in church would make Watergate burglars blush. That's the reason why the main work of the Church grinds to a halt in places while leaders seek to keep or gain control at any cost. Positional power, unless absolutely yielded to God's control, causes a downward spiral that diverts spiritual vitality away from the Church's mission. Those destructive steps often progress from manipulative domination to clutching control to bulldog stubbornness to a messiah obsession that deceives authoritarians into thinking they can do no wrong. All of this is in striking contrast to the way Jesus led.

### Misused Power Keeps a Church from Its Main Business

As church growth specialist Kent Hunter reminds us, all of this limits top-quality growth because it is the exact opposite of a church in which unbelievers see "the supernatural dynamic that shows the church to be a forgiving, loving, accepting group of people who themselves have been forgiven, loved and accepted by God through Jesus Christ."[10]

Astonishingly, even in stagnated or declining churches, power abusers seldom ask themselves, "Has my manipulation or control undermined dedication and lessened the interest of our members?" It's easier to blame the times or the lack of commitment of followers. The negative results are easy for others to see, however. New people are repulsed by power grabbing. Involved believers, though they may not leave, stand back to see what the controller can achieve alone. Discouraging results follow.

## Misused Power Undermines a Leader's Relationship to Christ

Greed for power can be sly, elusive, and startling to one who loves the power. Like most evils, it always takes one farther than the person intended to go. A leader should suspect his or her soul health when tempted to manipulate procedures, money, situations, and beliefs for selfish advantage. When this germ gets a toehold in one's soul, a raging fever follows. Next comes a delirium that makes a leader believe position, ordination, or status equals being special, smart, or spiritual. It is a frightening joke to think that superior insight or supernatural spirituality comes wrapped in a package labeled "power." It doesn't. To paraphrase Aleksandr Solzhenitsyn, "The meaning of earthly existence lies not, as we have grown used to thinking, in holding power but in the development of our soul."

## Misused Power Betrays Sacred Trusts

All authority, great or small, is a holy trust. Every leader on every level of church life must remember that he or she is charged with pleasing the Commanding Officer (2 Tim. 2:4). Since all leadership opportunities are a sacred stewardship from God, a power abuser is violating a trust that sabotages the cause it was meant to help.

A leader who wants to please God takes Richard Foster's admonition to heart: "Pride makes us think we are right, and power gives us the ability to cram our vision of rightness down everyone's throat. This marriage between pride and power carries us to the brink of the demonic."[11] What an accurate observation! The news, however, is not all bad. Authority can be used in Christ-exalting ways. God stands ready to join in a magnificent partnership with a leader who seeks His guidance and is willing to do God's work in His way. Authentic Christians love to follow those who lead as true servants. And the results are grand. Use of authority that satisfies the Father helps rather than harms, accepts rather than rejects, loves rather than maneuvers, and gives rather than takes.

## Misused Power Forgets Who Is Lord

Quaker Elton Trueblood warned, "Because we tend to forget the word *minister* means servant, there is always the temptation to reintroduce into Christian society the very standard which Christ explicitly rejected."[12] Mistakenly, many human leaders want to control what Christ alone rules. Scripture is clear: the Church has only one Lord, and that is Jesus Christ.

One writer raised the question "Why do we resist papal authority but settle for a miniature pope in many congregations, sometimes an unordained one at that?" Let's state the case more clearly. In place of ruling supremacy, Jesus offers poverty of spirit and self-giving service. His pattern is humility. Asbury Theological Seminary Professor Jerry Mercer underlines the issue: "Christ is the paradox of the last being first, the host waiting on tables, the slave being in charge. His is a leadership that believes in the beatitudes and self-denial, cross-bearing and faithful following. And it is leadership that transcends spiritual gifts—except for the one gift that really matters in the long run: the gift of love."[13]

## Misused Power Sees the Church as a Business

Among the Church's most pressing current problems is the corporate leadership model in the Church, which so thoroughly undermines the servant model of Jesus. Hierarchical structures of leadership like government or corporations encourage individuals to aim for the top. Meanwhile, the New Testament teaches us to value self-giving at the bottom. The business world urges us to promote ourselves, but Christ calls us to die to ourselves. Society suggests we get all we can, but the Kingdom calls us to give all we can. The corporation model wants control, profit, and production, while the Kingdom calls us to freedom in Christ, love at any cost, and fulfilling relationships among the people of God.

When a church views itself as a commercial enterprise, it quickly deteriorates into a mere dollars-and-cents venture in which well-intended idealists think they work for Christ but live far from His presence and power.

## WILL WE ACCEPT POWER GLUTTONY OR INITIATE CORRECTIONS?

Finding a cure for the power pestilence could help us renew the Church's mission and reenergize her evangelism. Recognizing the need to give up power-grasping tactics and fully embrace selfless servanthood forces leaders to make personal changes that could lead to renewal. The question before us is "How can leaders refocus the use of power on the living Lord of the Church?"

• **Resist infallibility.** Election, seniority, or status do not produce infallibility, such as the pope claims. To lead effectively, one must cultivate humility, which Thomas Mann's comical statement puts in perspective: "The good Lord sees your heart, not the braid on your jacket; before him we are all in our birthday suits, admirals and common men alike."[14] The person who uses leadership authority to exalt Christ feels like a fellow pilgrim with every other Christian. That person acts like a guest in the Master's house, whose primary task is to show others the way to the Father's banquet table.

• **Avoid ownership obsessions.** Glaring power-abuser symptoms appear when a leader uses possessive terms like "my church," "my calling," "my people," and "my ministry." Meanwhile, Jesus used two convincing pronouns, "I" and "my," in His promise "I will build my church" (Matt. 16:18). Those last five words from the Master keep us aware that He owns everything related to the Church.

All who aspire to be ecclesiastical leaders must heed these demanding words of Jesus: "You know that the rulers of the Gentiles lord it over them, and their high officials exercise authority over them. Not so with you. Instead, whoever wants to become great among you must be your servant, and whoever wants to be first must be your slave" (Matt. 20:25-27). Later, Paul testified about his own leadership practices, "Not that we lord it over your faith, but we work with you for your joy, because it is by faith you stand firm" (2 Cor. 1:24).

Peter underscores this ownership issue in another scriptural setting: "Be shepherds of God's flock that is under your care, serving as overseers—not because you must, but because you are willing, as God wants you to be; not greedy for money, but eager to serve; *not lording it over those entrusted to you, but being examples to the flock*" (1 Pet. 5:2-3, emphasis added).

• **Practice self-emptying.** Jesus put a new face on authority when He traded splendor for servanthood. Paul says He "emptied himself, taking the form of a servant, being born in the likeness of men" (Phil. 2:7, RSV). On all levels of church life this perspective must be rekindled. Our Lord's pattern for those who lead is carefully explained in that Philippian passage: leaders do not grasp for God's equality (v. 6), they empty themselves (v. 7), they commit to being a servant (v. 7), they humble themselves (v. 8), and they become obedient unto death (v. 8). The King James Version gives insightful meaning to self-emptying when it says Jesus "made himself of no reputation" (v. 7, KJV).

Such a view of authority sounds like a foreign language when compared to secular culture, which has so profoundly influenced the Church. Aggressive self-expression, coercive anger, stubborn dominance, calculated intimidation, and money-driven success is what the world wants and the Church cannot tolerate. But Jesus offers a powerful solution to this conflict: "The greatest among you will be your servant. For whoever exalts himself will be humbled, and whoever humbles himself will be exalted" (Matt. 23:11-12). In the previous sentence our Lord warned, "Never be called masters, for you have one master, the Christ" (v. 10, RSV). These passages make it abundantly clear that God neither wants privileged class nor recognizes an organizational elite in His Church.

• **Live agape.** Evidence of power abuse frequently shows in the way leaders think about and treat followers. Power addicts usually assume subordinates are flawed in some way and predestined to serve them. At the same time, these leaders view themselves as special because they hold position. As a result, the abuser often treats others as second-rate rather than regarding all members of God's family as equals and friends. Scripture teaches we are all fellow citizens of heaven and equally valued by the Head of the Church.

Paul's view of relationships between those with authority and followers shows in two clear-as-dawn sentences: "He died for all, that those who live should no longer live for themselves but for him who died for them and was raised again. *So from now on we regard no one from a worldly point of view*" (2 Cor. 5:15-16, emphasis added).

Agape—unmerited love and undeserved goodwill—is required by Christian leaders toward those they lead. This means authority holders must resist using counterfeit love to strengthen their control by telling followers "I love you" but never allowing agape to shape their behavior. Love costs effort, money, freedom, shared authority, affirmation, putting others first, and giving up ownership—counts on which selfish controllers are usually tightfisted.

• **Personify integrity.** The Pharisees had a habit of using high-sounding religious words to impress and gain prominence. In contrast, Jesus insisted that religious speech must be authenticated by lived-out love. Our Lord urged complete authenticity and modeling of Christian service when He said, "The teachers of the law and the Pharisees sit in Moses' seat. So you must obey them and do everything they tell you. But do not do what they do, for they do not practice what they preach. They tie up heavy loads and put them on men's shoulders, but they themselves are not willing to lift a finger to move them" (Matt. 23:2-4). Barclay summarizes this idea in a hard-hitting sentence: "Any religion which begets ostentation in action and pride in the heart is a false religion."[15]

Integrity and soul honesty are not flashy insignias to create good impressions. Rather, they are an outflow of the leader's connection with the Chief, which makes it possible for followers to see Jesus in such a person. They see Him as the leader prays, draws strength from a pure interior life, works to spiritually enrich his or her family, grows through adversity, and gives love to those who give mistreatment.

• **Avoid arrogance.** Paul teaches that humility starts with an accurate memory of who we used to be:

> Brothers, think of what you were when you were called. Not many of you were wise by human standards; not many were influential; not many were of noble birth. But God chose the foolish things of the world to shame the wise; God chose the weak things of the world to shame the strong. . . . It is because of him that you are in Christ Jesus, who has become for us wisdom from God—that is, our righteousness, holiness and redemption. Therefore, as it is written, "Let him who boasts boast in the Lord" (1 Cor. 1:26-27, 30-31).

The passage makes its own application to the contemporary church.

• **Refuse moral shortcuts.** Soon after settling into a position, officeholders can easily become hooked on the junk food of deal making—empty spiritual calories that contribute nothing to the health of the church or leader. Then in place of lofty victories, the person in charge chooses to accept expedient compromises—a dead-end street for spiritual vitality. A sobering example is Pilate, who, after examining the facts, concluded, "I find no fault in this man" (Luke 23:4, KJV). Then instead of principled action, Pilate polled his constituency. In turn, he gave them what they wanted with no consideration for what was right. He kept his position, but he will always be remembered as a moral coward.

Safety of position and moral compromises are the tempting way officeholders crucify the cause of Christ again in committee rooms, offices, pulpits, or in parking lot conversations after church services.

Our Lord's wilderness temptations record what He did when Satan seduced Him to take shortcuts with His authority. His temptation to transform stones into bread was a snare to fulfill personal needs—a common experience for all who lead.

Next, Jesus was enticed to create a sensational reputation by throwing himself down from the Temple. The enemy promised Jesus the kingdoms of the world. In the work of the Church, status tempts a leader much as Jesus was tempted. We can be enticed by selfish interest, tempted to take shortcuts to gain favor, or urged to try sensational actions to gain attention. But even when power dazzles or confuses us, the victory of Jesus provides strength and strategies to escape the enemy's traps. Our Lord's impressive wilderness examples shine helpful insight into every assignment in the Kingdom.

• **Welcome accountability.** Continuous character development plus accountability are two safeguards against the misuse of power. First Thess. 5:12 and Heb. 13:17 are often used by controllers to keep group members in line. Nearly everyone has heard these passages used to control others. However, demanding accountability for leaders stands at the center of the Thessalonian passage: "Now we ask you, brothers, to respect those who work hard among you, who are over you in the Lord and who admonish you. Hold them in the highest regard in love because of their work" (vv. 12-13). Before one gets to "highest regard," he or she must "work hard" and be "over you in the Lord."

Authority without accountability weakens most conscientious saints and often completely destroys mere pretenders.

Though power-hungry hirelings are often skilled at using high-sounding promises and frightening intimidation, God wants undershepherds to lead by what they have become by grace. Followers want the same, though they may not know how to verbalize it. Barclay helps us again: "It is not a question of personal prestige; but it is the task which makes a man great, and it is the service that he is doing that is his badge of honor."[16]

Accountability also shouts loud and clear in Heb. 13:17: "Obey your leaders and submit to their authority." So far, so good—leaders like that. But a requirement for leaders follows: "They keep watch over you as men who must give an account. Obey them so that their work will be a joy, not a burden, for that would be of no advantage to you." God requires accountability—they "must give an account"—of all who lead for Him.

It is important, then, for a leader to establish procedures to make himself accountable to the mission of the Church, to peers, and even to subordinates. Accountability often produces a surprisingly positive boomerang. When a leader increases accountability, voluntary accountability often goes up automatically throughout an entire organization.

Admittedly, the Church has many leaders who claim they are accountable to God and to a board of control. But in actual practice, many leaders fool themselves and their boards with a kind of rationalized distortion or fantasy. Try making yourself accountable to peers and subordinates for the use of your time, your effectiveness, your competency, your integrity, and your personal spiritual development. As a result, you will grow personally, and increased accountability among others will be a surprising by-product. David L. McKenna discusses the dynamics: "Accountability is a requirement for the Christian leader of the future which can only be achieved within the disciplines of confession and forgiveness that are exercised in the context of community."[17] The challenge and opportunity—initiate accountability to your peers and subordinates as well as your superiors.

Test your use of power against the scriptural standard of Ps. 15:

> Lord, who can be trusted with power,
>     And who may act in your place?
> Those with a passion for justice,
>     who speak the truth from their hearts;
> who have let go of selfish interests
>     and grown beyond their own lives;
> who see the wretched as their family
>     and the poor as their flesh and blood.
> They alone are impartial
>     and worthy of the people's trust.
> Their compassion lights up the whole earth,
>     and their kindness endures forever.[18]

### FINDING A CURE

Any biblical discussion of authority leaves little room

for anyone to feel self-righteous. Most leaders will some-times experience the temptations discussed in this chapter. Many succumb. Some resist with determined steadfastness. Others live all their lives near the edge. Nevertheless, warn-ings must be sounded, because power grasping always un-dermines ministry and undercuts redemptive service to Christ and His Church.

Could we reconsider a recovery plan patterned after a medical model? Here's how it works. Serious sickness re-quires more than examination and diagnosis. If health is to be restored, diagnosis must be followed with treatment—medication, surgery, or even chemotherapy.

In a similar manner, dealing with power temptations in one's leadership requires more than diagnosis. The healing starts with decisive obedience to question ourselves about all rationalizations of misused authority. Radical surgery may mean confession to wronged parties. Total recovery may de-mand repentance to God and those who have been injured by our lust for status.

Infected leaders, however, must move beyond mere cos-metic surgery to self-crucifixion, that Christ may receive the glory He deserves. Fast-growing egomania cells must be zapped with massive doses of accountability to God, peers, and the people who support Christian causes.

God's cure offers health and wellness for the individual and unlocks growth for the Church. Nouwen describes the kind of spiritually healthy people God can use: "Powerless-ness and humility in the spiritual life do not refer to people who have no spine and who let everyone else make decisions for them. These words refer to people who are so deeply in love with Jesus that they are ready to follow Him where He guides them, always trusting that, with Him, they will find life and find it abundantly."[19]

Christian authority, as we have seen, is exactly upside down from the way secular organizations use power. Samuel Logan Brengle clearly illuminates this issue: "The final esti-mate of men shows that history cares not an iota for the rank or title a man has borne, or the office he has held, but only the quality of his deeds and the character of his mind and heart."[20]

Revitalized spiritual and numerical growth can flow again like life-giving oxygen into the Body of Christ when all authority is yielded to His Lordship and then shared with followers. The apostle Paul uses six short words to nail down these issues: "Strength is for service, not status" (Rom. 15:1, TM).

# 7

# Power—Resource for a Leader's Inner World

## Being Comes Before Doing

The world and the church have a right to expect religious leaders to be Christlike. But a human leader is powerless to exemplify wholehearted fidelity and unquestionable integrity without the Holy Spirit's enablement. And this divine resourcing must be personal before it starts showing in Kingdom achievement.

God empowers Christ's traits in us when we allow Him to do so. Christian writer A. W. Tozer underscored this issue nearly half a century ago when he advised, "God can use anyone, however flawed, if the vessel is clean." That exhortation is uncommonly insightful for our times, because too many Christian leaders confuse image with character and have incredibly compromised the cause of Christ in the process.

### GOD'S POWER MAKES US RIGHT INSIDE

An old country preacher stated the case accurately: "Some of you are so busy *doing* something, you ain't *been* nothing yet." He is absolutely right—authentic Kingdom achievements must be rooted in moral purity and personal piety. Being must come before doing and motivate our doing. Personal authenticity and moral cleanness stand at the top of God's requirements for a leader. A holy life is always more important than reputation, scholarship, genius, and experience.

But Sam Keen, in his book *To a Dancing God,* describes our dilemma when he writes of his own discovery: "The sanctity required of me was not within the range of my will power."[1]

## Supernatural Power for Purity

Personal purity, when it permeates every dimension of the human personality, is a vivid example of human weakness transformed by God's strength. No one can be truly pure without God's help. Neither can one pull oneself up to moral cleanness by the bootstraps. From Christian history, however, we see inspiring examples of persons who possessed personal purity whom the Spirit made bigger than life, stronger than their imperfections, and more principled than their own egos. To borrow Pippert's idea, the Holy Spirit made them "worthy of being mimed."[2] What an unbeatable combination—our best plus our complete dependence connects us to God's supernatural empowerment.

Robert Murray McCheyne, the godly young Scottish divine, summarized the issue so well: "A holy minister is an awful weapon in the hands of a holy God." Sadly, the opposite is true, too—power in the hand of a leader who is not pure triggers disarray, leads to corruption, and brings the church to a standstill. It is hard to imagine what the results might be if 500 religious leaders in North America waited before God for a moral and spiritual overhaul, even if it required a 10-day focused wait as the disciples had in the Upper Room. And what would happen if the pastor and 5 to 10 lay leaders in every church did the same?

## Supernatural Power Fuels Active Goodness

God intends that empowered piety would motivate amazing action. Though religious isolation has often paralyzed world evangelization for almost 2,000 years, real spirituality leads to energetic ministry to the world.

God honors all believers by calling them to meaningful involvement in redeeming lost people. This involvement may be much like my grandson who, when he was four years of age, helped vacuum the carpet. You have the picture—though he actually helped very little, his effort gave him a sense of participation. He didn't do much to clean the floors. What we do for God is like that—He could easily get along without us, but we need to be involved with Him. Such involvement makes us better, and He honors our feeble efforts with magnificent results.

## Supernatural Power to Grow in Love

Everyone, even the unlovely, craves love. Church growth research shows that love attracts people to any church. Life in our high-tech and low-touch society makes contemporary people need affirming love more than ever. Many secular people are spiritually and emotionally starved because they live loveless lives. God plans for every believer to be rich by giving and receiving love.

On a *Love Care Quotient Survey*, 8,600 church members were asked, "Using a scale of 1 to 10, how loved do you feel by members of your church?" Church growth consultant Win Arn summarizes the results of the research: "Their responses were compared to the growth of their churches, and a clear relationship emerged. People feel more loved in growth churches than in declining churches."

Concerning this relation between love and church growth, Arn urged, "Raising the 'love-ability' of your church will have far greater impact on reaching new people than better sermons, new facilities, more parking, and additional programs. Love is the foundation of all other principles of growth."[3]

Love, the captivating way Jesus attracted people, reached a perfect expression in Him. Our Lord demonstrated love all along His earthly journey, especially at Calvary. Consequently, He is the love pattern for our lives and our churches. Love nourishes human relationships so well that many top corporate CEOs now promote it as an important growth ingredient for businesses. In the church and community, the love of Christ renews people, warms entire congregations, and attracts outsiders.

Love has had top priority on the Christian agenda from the start. Our Lord declared, "By this shall all men know that ye are my disciples, if ye have love one to another" (John

13:35, KJV). Evidently Jesus expected disciples to love folks, even those who scorned or mistreated them. He calls us to a love that is deeper than fuzzy feelings for congenial people. His love standards still apply, but without divine empowerment really caring for the unlovely is impossible.

Thus leaders on all levels of the Church are called to be living examples of the magnetic possibilities and incredible strengths that are built into Paul's well-read message: "Love is patient, love is kind, and is not jealous; love does not brag and is not arrogant, does not act unbecomingly; it does not seek its own, is not provoked, does not take into account a wrong suffered, does not rejoice in unrighteousness, but rejoices with the truth; bears all things, believes all things, hopes all things, endures all things" (1 Cor. 13:4-7, NASB). Paul lived love and recommended love as a way of life. He knew that everyone who practiced the love of Jesus would be an influential spokesperson for Christ and in the process find great fulfillment as a human being.

The love chapter, 1 Cor. 13, portrays the kind of love we gladly receive but find difficult to give. Thoughtful disciples will ask, "Who could love to the extent this scripture admonishes us?" The answer—only persons filled with divine enablement can love to such an outrageous length and depth. But we can do it with God's help, and many will be drawn to Christ because of our love for them.

## Supernatural Power to Accept Yourself

Just as human survival requires inhaling and exhaling, self-surrender and self-love are two essential spiritual components of God's interior development for us. The Holy Spirit empowers two needed realities of self-acceptance—self-renunciation and self-esteem. Apparently it is spiritually lopsided to have one without the other.

Both self-renunciation and self-esteem occurred in the disciples during their last meal with Jesus. After they were completely humbled by the Lord's washing their feet, they found it hard to be arrogant or proud again. That event boggled their thoughts about themselves and about the future of

Christianity. Think of it—the Lord of glory took a basin and towel to wash their feet—that humbled them. At the same time, our Lord's unconditional acceptance of the disciples and His outspoken need of them made them know they were valued in the Kingdom—that built their self-esteem.

Consider this balancing reality. Self-surrender and self-acceptance, taken together, form a life-giving root system for appropriate self-love. Thus, though we are unworthy of what God did for us in Christ, we are sons and daughters in His family with all the privileges, relationships, and responsibilities. The Spirit's enablement makes us key players in the Father's efforts to redeem His world, though we are nothing in ourselves.

Consequently, I have no reason to think of myself as inferior or superior. The act of centering my life in Christ moves my focus from self to God. This means that any diligent follower of Christ can accept himself or herself without condemnation or without exaltation.

This is good news. Our self-image draws strength from our relationship to Jesus, so we are no longer slaves to a mulish past, inferiority feelings, or emotional abuse. This means too that we can enjoy realistic self-esteem because of who we are becoming in relation to Christ.

## GOD'S POWER TURNS THE WORLD RIGHT SIDE UP

An uproar happened at Thessalonica shortly after the dawn of the Early Church. Paul and Silas gave accusers many reasons to conclude, "The men, . . . who are reducing the whole civilized order of things to chaos, have arrived here too" (Acts 17:6, BARCLAY). When one considers the size of the early Christian group, their communication limitations, and slow travel, this reputation is amazing. Their secret—they were empowered within before they tried to go out.

Incredibly enough, these protests in this verse proved prophetic. Christianity, inaugurated by this tiny, politically powerless group of disciples, spilled out of a tightly locked upstairs dining room into the streets of Jerusalem. On their way to taking Christ to cities, villages, and the backwaters of the world, the Holy Spirit resourced them to do more than any group of any size had ever done before. Their critics were right: they were holy, energized troublemakers.

Their inner transformation was fully as amazing as their increased influence on their world. Bigotry was purged. Rivalry for position was cleansed from their hearts. They faced martyrdom without fear. Their wills, fired by the Spirit of God, inspired them to attempt extraordinary missionary ministries where they had been filled earlier with feelings of self-pity, inadequacy, and provincialism. Then the Holy Spirit made them miraculously adequate, so they astounded themselves and impacted their world with the gospel.

### Supernatural Power to Speak

Though witnessing by definition requires speaking, a convincing Christian witness needs to be more than a good talker. Well-placed silence for Jesus can sometimes speak more loudly than words. But there's no doubt that words do possess power. They have power to strengthen and renew. They discourage or excite. They browbeat or bless. Just now I can easily recall a gentle word of grace spoken 50 years ago by my grandmother, though my mental picture of her has grown dim. This morning I was drawn to the Savior when I sang a song Charles Wesley wrote over 200 years ago. Strong words stay with us. And with God's help, I too may speak a word today that may motivate action long after my voice has been stilled in death.

The opposite is also true. A destructive word may dishearten someone, perhaps forever. I can grouse to gain sympathy but cause those who hear to give up hope. Even the wrong tone of voice sometimes keeps someone away from Christ.

Our Lord had the power of words in mind when He promised enablement to speak in His name—even in faraway places the disciples had only heard about and to strange people they had never met.

Words change lives, shape society, and alter the course of history. Winston Churchill, Franklin Roosevelt, and Adolf Hitler are examples. The Bible is also filled with model witnesses who impacted the world, and we still marvel at what their words accomplished. Maybe our Lord was thinking about their upcoming sermons in Acts when the Early Church leaders spoke so passionately about His resurrection. Possibly our Lord was thinking about the holy boldness the first disciples would show in speaking before the Sanhedrin when they announced, "Judge for yourselves whether it is right in God's sight to obey you rather than God. For we cannot help speaking about what we have seen and heard" (Acts 4:19-20). Conceivably, Jesus might have had the coming judgment of Ananias and Sapphira in mind when well-deserved, condemning words showed how much greed and self-centeredness they harbored in their hearts (5:3-4, 9). Or perhaps He anticipated a word of encouragement you uttered yesterday to a hurting friend.

Think of the possibilities. At this very moment, the Father may be searching for a fervent prophet for the new century. Then again, He may be looking for a nonblustery, unpretentious spokesperson to speak quietly in your office, factory, or community.

Healing for moral tongue-tiedness is needed now more than ever. The One who nudged Moses to speak for Him is prodding us with His message, "Who gave man his mouth? Who makes him deaf or mute? . . . Now go; I will help you speak and will teach you what to say" (Exod. 4:11-12). Supernatural speech is so needed in contemporary culture. Now is a significant time to speak up for righteousness in our homes, schools, workplaces, courtrooms, media, public forums, churches, magazines, political campaigns, and on television and radio. Why not speak up for the Savior wherever friends and neighbors gather, regardless of whether or not they are Christian?

Speak up for Christ. You have a lot to say because of whose you are and because of what He has done in you.

## Supernatural Power to Do More than You Think You Can

Washing feet and waiting tables are as much a part of sharing the gospel as preaching and teaching. Servanthood is needed in many expressions of Christian service, but grace and commitment to serve in humble assignments do not come automatically or naturally. Such willingness to do the less prominent expressions of service comes from the Holy Spirit's enablement.

Servanthood in the Kingdom is an amazingly varied proposition with important work for everyone. In its finest expression, servanthood—being a love slave for Christ—humbles the mighty, exalts the meek, and changes the world.

Equipping enablement might take a believer to highly visible missionary service in an exotic place. It might mean a Christian statesperson would have a global influence in national or international halls of government. It might even energize a scientific genius at the cutting edge of medical research. Or it may mean a trusted position in a local congregation.

God's enablement, on the contrary, sometimes shuts us up to serve in a quiet place of prayer, assigns us to uncelebrated work in a hospice, or directs us to become Sunday School teachers to the next generation. Wesley understood the full range of this idea when he prayed, "Let me be employed by You or laid aside for You." Supernatural enablement is required for both.

This power, with its countless expressions, puts to rest the false notion that one individual can't have a phenomenal effect in our world. Every generation needs more like Tom Dooley, Martin Luther King Jr., Mother Teresa, Albert Schweitzer, Dwight Moody, or Dag Hammarskjöld. And who can even imagine the impact some unknown prayer partner had on these highly visible servants of God to help them do such heroic feats for Him? The Father wants many new names, including yours, added to the list of achievers or behind-the-scenes encouragers.

### Supernatural Power to See

God always has more remarkable things going on in His world than we normally see. This divine power, provided in the midst of ordinary life, makes us see many things much more clearly. Divine aid helps believers see unique Kingdom opportunities, expands their perspective, or helps them see their world in new ways. All this has surprised disciples by what God had planned for their next move. And it also helps us see ourselves as He sees us.

When the Spirit touched their ways of seeing, the perspectives of those first-century believers cleared like the morning sun drives night away. A fresh enduement helped them see Christ to be the Messiah, the Anointed One, God's Son. They were empowered to help those who heard their witnessing, teaching, and preaching see wonderful new truth about God. This power to see more and farther erupted into a propelling force for righteousness and became a beacon of high-quality living. And it still is.

New perspectives helped them produce impressive church growth as they recovered from their cultural baggage and religious blindness.

An extraordinary example of 20/20 spiritual vision shows in Philip's actions and reactions and God-usefulness at Samaria. Soon after fleeing for his life from Jerusalem, as a lay leader Philip opened the gospel to Samaritans. What a startling new viewpoint—to open the gospel to a nationality hated by the Jews! In a few days the Holy Spirit used the same revival to test the culturally ingrained prejudices of Peter and John, two prominent headquarters trendsetters from the church at Jerusalem. As happens so often, those closest to the trenches of ministry saw the greatest opportunities. Philip saw what God was doing long before Peter and John did.

Samaria produced a whole new way of seeing, which pushed the Church out of its frightened cloisters into the world. God used an unlikely situation and an inexperienced, religiously naive lay leader named Philip as "the hit man for the gospel." Just a short time later, through this same witness of Philip, the treasury secretary for Queen Candace of Ethiopia believed on Christ in an out-of-the-way, lonely place. These amazing, unanticipated outcomes resulted from the radically changing views God gave persons in the Early Church, especially Philip and Peter and John. God used

Philip as the spiritual spark plug for the Samaritans and the Africans.

After first-century believers received God's healing for blinding myopia, they used incredibly innovative strategies to impact their world for Christ. After God thoroughly tested Peter's stick-in-the-mud perspective, he started preaching about visions and dreams in an environment deeply steeped in religious tradition. It was as if Peter was seeing the world through the eyes of God for the first time, and he could not keep the excitement to himself.

The Holy Spirit wants to do an extraordinary healing of our vision too. Consider the possibilities: What about the up-and-outers who need the gospel? Why not try to listen for the haunting cries coming from God-starved cities while we worship, do our service, and give our money in the suburbs? Ponder the spiritual despair of many in deserted rural places. And what response will we give to the hungry, empty-souled secularist who works at the next computer terminal or lives next door?

But there is much more. Even as this power must certainly make us see the possibilities of numerical and geographical expansion, it also helps us see the expansion of the Kingdom into unclaimed places like government, science, and culture.

Crisp, clear, Christ-centered, contemporary messages delivered by new-way-of-seeing disciples will be a victorious match for what keeps churches from changing the world for Christ. Clearer vision is needed now more than ever before.

## Supernatural Power to Accomplish God's Purposes

The first century's revolutionary Christian impact on self and society must be regained. Columnist Cal Thomas summarizes what has been lost and what needs to be recaptured: "The church once had power: moral power, spiritual power, the power to transform not only people's lives but also to heal society's deepest ills. That power, as the history of this and other countries has revealed, is greater than any government, no matter how much money government spends or how many points of light it seeks to illuminate on its own."[4] Earlier in the same editorial, Thomas's analysis observes that our contemporary situation is desperate, and it is. Every believer can identify more than one moral logjam in society or the Church that needs to be dynamited. And who will do it if it is not done by believers?

Regrettably, no one seems to know how or where to start. Or is it fear? Few people want to rock the boat in the Church or disturb things in the world, so we have inaction and silence. No one likes to be labeled as a troublemaker, so we have surrendered to be mesmerized by those who most need us, even though they may not know it. Many don't know what to do about our contemporary gospel challenges, because so few have seen corrections accomplished with a loving Christian spirit. And blind compliance is often highly valued as a Christian virtue. But such a status quo produces a Church that remains comfortably undisturbed, reasonably well scrubbed, and pitifully trivial.

Though the moral logjams vary from place to place, there is much that needs to be done. The list is long. Sins must be named. Corruption must be confronted. Voters must voice their convictions at the polls. One-to-one evangelism must be implemented. Spiritual renewal must be experienced. Moral integrity must be proclaimed and lived. Baby Christians must be assimilated into the churches. Intercessory prayer must be rekindled. Lavish stewardship must be revived. Damaging inertia must be confronted and changed. New churches must be planted. Pontificating leaders must be forced to forthright accountability. Manipulation must be stopped. And churches must grow, spiritually and numerically.

## DO WE UNDERSTAND THE POTENTIAL BEFORE US?

Could it be that the Father wants to begin reviving His Church through us? I think the answer is a resounding *yes*. Why not pray that holy enablement will shape you, your church, your community, your country, and even your world into what God wants it to be? Does it sound too much for you? Good! That's where supernatural enablement always starts. It begins when a believer sees what needs to be done and admits his or her personal powerlessness to do anything.

Can one person or a small group make a difference? The answer is *yes.* Jesus started with 12, and one of them defected as a traitor.

Dare to believe and dream what this supernatural energy can do through you in our time. Who thought the Berlin Wall would be battered into rubble in our time? Who really believed that Communism's ironclad grip could be broken? Both took place within a year. I confess that I prayed with hope that it might happen in a generation or two. But the catastrophic world changes in Berlin and Russia encourage me to believe that God can do mighty things for His Church in a much shorter time span than many of us think. Strongholds of the enemies of the cause of Christ can be broken down just as the Berlin Wall came down.

God's strength, the holy enablement we need, comes in response to our willingness to put our fervor, stamina, vision, wealth, status, and egos on the line for His use. It is this power for achievement from beyond that inspired Paul's affirmation, "I can do all things through Christ which strengtheneth me" (Phil. 4:13, KJV). Service to Christ and the needs of persons around us is God's miraculous deliverance from selfish self-interest. It is the indescribable joy of putting the cause of Christ at the center of our dreams, priorities, and lifestyles.

The contemporary Church already holds what it needs in its hand—ecclesiastical power, gifted personnel, competent leadership, impressive facilities, prestige, respectability, money, and organization. But it needs one more thing—a supernatural empowerment of all its personnel at every level, and I mean *every* level.

As never before, the contemporary Church needs the renewed, invincible fire of God at her spiritual center, to make her a redemptive instrument for converting the world to faith in Jesus Christ. The time has arrived to refuse to be fooled by the seductions from the superficial. It is time to kindle a flame of genuine righteousness. It is time to denounce sin in high and low places. It is time to pray, praise, plead, fast, and pledge. Our commission from God includes the whole world. A divine enablement for a lifestyle revolution and church-changing renewal is promised by the Father. Such a wholehearted commitment by God and us to such a lofty cause has the potential to keep us fired up for a lifetime.

Let's intercede for ourselves, for our peers, and for our churches:

Lord, let your Spirit give me power
    to overcome all hesitation,
    to take away all fear,
        and to remove all shyness.
May your Spirit help me
    respond gratefully to you,
    speak freely about you to everyone I meet,
        and act courageously to let your Kingdom come.[5]

—Henri Nouwen

# 8

# Service—a Cause Well Worth Living For

## *Lessons from the Towel*

Servants' Entrance are the words on a handmade sign over the entrance to St. Bede's Episcopal Church in Santa Fe, New Mexico.[1] Every church could post a similar sign to remind worshipers that servanthood is a satisfying, nonnegotiable requirement of Christianity. Those words—"servants' entrance"—challenge every disciple to fully grasp the amazing fact that every effort done for Christ has potential power to change the world. Those two words challenge Jesus' followers to authentic Christlikeness.

The words on the sign also remind us that Christ is our constant Enabler in every attempt we make to serve as His voice and hands in our corner of the world. I need to be reminded often of the supernatural dimensions of service. I need Bede's sign to remember my service for Christ needs frequent examination and evaluation. I love the message of it so much that I hope the gates of heaven will have such a sign.

Several assumptions need to be discussed as a foundation for understanding the supernatural dimensions of service. To get a fuller picture of how significant service is in the Bible, check how many columns it takes in your concordance to list words like "service," "servant," "serving," and "slave." In this interaction with Scripture, you will be especially attracted to the all-time Model for service—Jesus. Our Lord's life, death, and resurrection are inspiring examples of serving, even when the cost is gigantic. As He said, the Son of God came to serve and not to be served. In concise, easy-to-understand words, service is taking what you have been given and spending it on others.

## LESSONS FROM THE TOWEL

I'm always humbled by the mental picture of our Lord washing feet in the Upper Room. Think of it—He demonstrated service at a time when His mind was filled with issues of obedience and His will was challenged by sacrifice. Think of the realities—while facing terrible betrayal, denial by His disciples, and death for the sins of humanity, He stooped to show the disciples how to serve. The biblical passage underscores the magnificent miracles and mysteries of service when it says, "Jesus knowing that the Father had given all things into his hands . . . began to wash the disciples' feet" (John 13:3, 5, KJV).

Scripture also teaches that servants in every generation are the greatest natural resource of Christianity. And concerning our reasons for serving—acts of service never guarantee merit with God, nor do they give us a ticket to heaven.

• **Gift to God.** Service is a love gift to God that expresses our devotion to Him through our commitment, energy, and the effort of our hands and feet. Service is God's purpose for a human being lived out with joy in the day-by-day relationships of life. Elizabeth O'Connor, faithful laywoman and author from the Church of the Savior in Washington, D.C., explains why we must connect inner piety and outward service: "Every inward work requires an outward expression or the inner work comes to naught. In fact, non-service may fracture us further, widening the split between what we inwardly subscribe to and what we outwardly do."[2] She is right. A servant's perspective helps us meet God in the people we serve. But there is more.

• **A gift God gives us.** Every Kingdom assignment, though the logic appears critically flawed to secularists, is also a gift from God to us. It is His exercise program given to keep us spiritually fit and to increase our capacity for righteousness. These "soul calisthenics" give us insights from people we serve, develop a new realism about our abilities and gifts, underscore new demands we read in the Scriptures, and make us more aware of the needs of people around us.

• **Addiction to activity isn't service.** The downside of serving happens when treadmills of activity are initiated or continued for our own gratification. How can that be? It happens when a person fools himself or herself into believing he or she is Christ-motivated when actually being self-motivated. In such a state of mind, the individual becomes addicted to activity.

Service done for the wrong reason usually turns into empty self-righteousness. Then a person uses a service assignment to elevate his or her reputation, ego, or business. This disease of the soul causes a rush of activities that do not nourish the activist at a deep spiritual level. Self-centered service finally leads to frustration, bitterness, and abandoning the cause altogether.

Service, as we have seen, is a gift we give God and a gift He gives us. This giving and receiving reminds me of a child with $1.87 shopping for a gift for her mother costing $50.00. The little girl asks her aunt, "Aunt Karen, would you like to chip in with me?"

• **More than inconvenient duty.** Service is intended by God to be a delight more than a duty. Ideally the question should not be "Do I have to?" but "Why does He trust me with this?" Secular *Newsweek* columnist Marian Wright Edelman quietly preaches a significant sermon to Christians when she called service "the rent you pay for living, not something you do in your spare time."[3]

Why serve as a duty when one could be energized by love? Maybe doing something as a duty is better than not doing it, but it is a lot more enjoyable teaching a class, preaching a sermon, or making a hospital call for the love of it.

Apparently the greater the demands an assignment requires, the more people are willing to try it. In his memorable inaugural address, United States President John F. Kennedy underscored this biblical principle, though he probably didn't realize it, when he called Americans to ask what they could do for their country, not what their country could do for them. The challenge of accomplishing hard stuff for Christ is apparently the reason many believers are often motivated to accomplish colossal achievements for God.

• **Service given = service received.** For wholehearted disciples, love for Christ motivates action, stimulates creativity, challenges commitment. Love for the Master sets forces, choices, relationships, and crises in motion that provide unimaginable possibilities and produce incredible accomplishments. While service is usually thought to be an action we do for someone else, it often turns into a boomerang that enriches those who serve. Consequently, service gives us opportunity to impact others while it shapes and enriches us. Service given is service received: comfort and you are comforted; cheer and you are cheered; teach and you are taught; give and you receive; love and you are loved.

• **Service need not be complicated.** Incredible satisfactions from service can be found everywhere. Even the simplest deed often impacts another person forever. Recently I saw sheer delight in two children's eyes, ages 9 and 11, whose parents take them on a regular basis to serve food to the homeless at the Los Angeles Mission. On the surface, such a small act seems almost too trifling to discuss. But consider the results. Family togetherness grew around a Jesus lifestyle. Street people enjoyed the children—a blessing generally not available to them. Overtaxed mission workers were assisted. And no one can imagine the rippling effect of these events on the children when they reach 39 and 41; perhaps they will be benefactors, volunteers, or even directors of a mission.

This means a common assumption needs to be rethought. Too many believers consider nonspectacular acts of caring and compassion as unimportant or insignificant. Not so. Try reconsidering the amazing potential in every act of service for Christ. Service can be significant and eternal whether it is big or trivial, impressive or mundane, distinct or unnoticed, noble or nebulous. Rosa Parks had no idea that a refusal to move to the rear of the bus would make her a household name and fu-

el a movement for equality and justice in our country; she had
no idea she was serving a cause that would change the social
fabric of the nation. The results of service can never be mea-
sured by how important it seems at first.

Consider an example that moved me deeply. In one of
my classes, an adult student told about teaching his seven-
year-old daughter how to enjoy serving others without any
thought of applause. One afternoon he took his daughter and
20 dimes to feed expired parking meters in downtown Colorado Springs. They left little notes on windshields telling
auto owners they had kept them from receiving a ticket and
explaining they felt motivated by love for people and Jesus.
On the way home, father and daughter enjoyed discussing
how auto owners must have felt as they returned to their
cars. They also had a good laugh together about how
shocked the meter maid might have been.

But ponder this unanticipated payoff—the little girl remarked with an "aha" insight: "Daddy, we had more fun
than anyone, didn't we?" While I have no way of knowing
whether or not car owners were gripped by this random act
of kindness, I believe the girl will never forget the experience. Two dollars in dimes and her dad's imagination will
enrich her service for Christ across her lifetime. What a small
investment—a short walk, 20 dimes, and a dash of creativity
by her dad—for such a potential result.

Even when an act of service seems small to us, when it is
done right for the right reason it pleases our Lord. The one
who does much in a small class, church, or community pleases God more than a person with a bigger opportunity who
does little or nothing.

We enjoy an incredibly satisfying serendipity when we
begin to discover that service reaches beyond our lifetime
and beyond our awareness; we must be reminded often that
service sometimes blesses and transforms persons we will
never meet. For example, in a men's growth group I attend
with prospective pastors, every new idea and serious commitment made by members of the group will ultimately impact people they will serve wherever they go and however

long they serve. Serving reaches beyond anything we could ever imagine.

And service has its own rewards. Beverly Sills, New York opera star and a volunteer for the March of Dimes, recommended giving oneself without getting a dinner, tote bag, or T-shirt. Then she continued, "The volunteer who holds out a hand, be it manicured or calloused, bejeweled or gnarled, black, white, yellow, or red, becomes a shareholder in the lives of her fellow human beings."

## SERVICE MAKES US ARCHITECTS OF THE ENDURING

Christianity is service from beginning to end; it is service given, service received, and service that satisfies. All authentic followers of our Lord serve because of their love for Him—a response in direct opposition to salvation by works. Southern Baptist Evangelist Vance Havner loved to remind his hearers, "While we sing about the price Jesus paid, we might check on what God expects from us, not to repay Him, but as an expression of our heart's love to Him who redeemed us."[4] Love motivates service.

• **Rooted in grateful hearts.** Selfless service to Christ is motivated by the astonishment we feel about Christ—who He is, what He does for us, and how He continually shapes us into His lovely image. Effective service has deep roots in a grateful heart. Such thankfulness for Christ molds our character, commitment, and competency.

Serving others in Christ's name and for His glory is a wonderful way we become something beautiful for God. The phrase "something beautiful for God" comes from Mother Teresa of Calcutta. She purposefully makes misery and affliction into something beautiful for the Lord. Maybe a similar thing is possible in every limited situation in the world, including power-battered tiny churches, urban settings blighted by the consequences of sin, and declining established churches. To neglect these amazing benefits of service guarantees a shallow, lonely life. Kingdom service affords incredible satisfactions—seek them with your whole heart.

• **Made for each other.** More and more I am coming to

believe that God made us for others, and others were made for us. Scientist Albert Einstein's perspective needs to be meaningfully accepted and practiced by every Christian: "A hundred times every day, I remind myself that my inner and outer life are based on the labors of other men, living and dead, and that I must exert myself in order to give in the same measure as I have received."[5] Though giving ourselves in the measure we receive is a very big order, trying to do so expands the soul. An amazing secret of Christian service is at work—service is good for the servant.

Service, in a basic sense, means caring for what and whom God cares about, and that includes everyone. It focuses our interests outside ourselves. It unites our fragmented selves as it challenges our all-too-common self-centered preoccupations about ourselves and our world. Service is an adventure in caring and compassion and grace that sometimes turns into the most exciting game in town.

• **Does God really need us?** Christian service, bottom line, is an opportunity God gives us rather than a favor we do for Him. Many forget that the One who created the world can get along well without our service. At Athens Paul preached, "The God who made the world and everything in it, this Master of sky and land, doesn't live in custom-made shrines or *need the human race to run errands for him, as if he couldn't take care of himself*" (Acts 17:25, TM, emphasis added). But what satisfaction we experience when we give ourselves to make a significant difference in someone else's small world.

• **Service enriches those who serve.** Service for Christ may have high visibility like the efforts of Mother Teresa or Billy Graham or James Dobson. Or it may be more unknown, like the efforts of Mary or Ted or Sam, who serve in the church nursery or scrub the church rest rooms. Service need not be highly visible to be significant.

American poet Ralph Waldo Emerson might have been reading Scripture for his inspiration when he wrote, "It is one of the most beautiful compensations of this life that no one can sincerely try to help another without helping himself." In the biblical account of the helping Samaritan, every character was personally enriched except those who ignored the victim's plight. A similar experience happens in us—we are never the same, and always better, after giving ourselves to some costly, demanding service to a person, a cause, or *the* cause.

### SERVICE CHALLENGES ME TO BE CHRISTLIKE

A story comes from those dark years when the wall divided Berlin. Guards in East Berlin allowed a garbage truck through the wall, and it dumped a ton of rubbish in West Berlin. West Berliners responded by returning a truckload of canned food with a sign that read, "Let each give what he has to give." That's a parable for contemporary disciples— we give what we have to give, and it can change the world.

It's time to reenergize the soul of many contemporary churches and revolutionize our part of the world with righteousness. Service is a fruitful way to do it. Consider again what Jesus thought and taught us about serving. Listen closely to His teaching about service, as if you were hearing it for the first time.

- Service is to be done according to one's ability.
  "From everyone who has been given much, much will be demanded; and from the one who has been entrusted with much, much more will be asked" (Luke 12:48).
- Service is the cornerstone of Kingdom greatness.
  "Whoever wants to be first must be slave of all" (Mark 10:44).
- Service demonstrates the love of God.
  "Jesus said, 'Simon son of John, do you truly love me?' He answered, 'Yes, Lord, you know that I love you.' Jesus said, 'Take care of my sheep'" (John 21:16).
- Service often seems insignificant.
  "And if anyone gives even a cup of cold water to one of these little ones because he is my disciple, I tell you the truth, he will certainly not lose his reward" (Matt. 10:42).

- Service is modeled after Christ.
  "The Son of Man did not come to be served, but to serve, and to give his life as a ransom for many" (Matt. 20:28).
- Service must turn attention to God.
  "Let your light shine before men, that they may see your good deeds and praise your Father in heaven" (Matt. 5:16).

Since Christlikeness is my magnificent obsession, I work to know how my life looks to Jesus and duplicate what He would do in my circumstances. I want to go where Jesus would go if He lived in my neighborhood or town. I want to say what Jesus would say to people in my relationships, both intimate and professional. I want to give the way Jesus would give to the needs around me. I want to feel what Jesus would feel in my situation. This effort to be Christlike in all levels of living makes me more like Him and helps me serve others the way He served.

Service, as it calls me to wholehearted Christlikeness, challenges my attitudes about self and others so I can be free from needing to be "Mr. Strong" and "Mr. Be in Control." My intentional caring for others is God's cure for my me-first-ism. Yours too. Assisting others questions my self-pity as I meet overcomers who are victors with much bigger problems than mine. From these experiences and 10,000 like them, I have learned that serving is a wonderfully wholesome way to keep close to God—fully as effective as times of withdrawal and meditation.

Service also helps us know God believes in us. General Ulysses S. Grant was reported to have said to United States President Abraham Lincoln, "I was successful because you believed in me." A call to servanthood in the gospel means God trusts you with a part of His kingdom.

My friend Bob Benson, now with the Lord, wrote simply and profoundly about our service: "I think Jesus is saying to us, 'You're going out to serve. Don't take too good care of yourself, find something that counts, stick your neck out, spill some blood, spread some love.' . . . I am coming to believe the true meaning of our lives is in the touching and washing and smiling and lifting."[6]

While serving, my prayer becomes richer, the Bible lights up with amazing fresh inspiration, my experiences of fellowship take on deeper meaning, and my effectiveness in Kingdom tasks becomes more evident.

All this adds up to another miracle and mystery about service—the more I do for Christ, the more I really do believe He is the Savior of the world. That's the irony—hard work for the gospel reinforces my belief even as it deepens my commitments.

## TEN SHORT LESSONS ABOUT SERVICE

**1. People are the main reason we serve.** Scripture shows how precious people are to God. I wish they were always perfect, or at least nice. I wish they were always kind and never tried to complicate the life of Christian leaders. I wish they were all healthy, whole, and holy. It would be so much better if they were always agreeable, generous, and patient. But we all know problem-causing, needy people who are involved in the life of the Church. Service means giving ourselves to people, even the troubled ones. The commitment of the individual to Christian service is the lifeblood of the Christian cause.

**2. Not everyone serves in the same way.** The indwelling Christ creatively endows all of us for doing something important for God. Paul taught, "The gifts we possess differ as they are allotted to us by God's grace, and must be exercised accordingly" (Rom. 12:6, NEB). But everyone must do something—the servant of Christ holds a key to changing the neighborhood or the world.

**3. Participation increases commitment.** Robert Coles's phrase is powerful and true: "I think there is a lust for service in all of us."[7] Everyone needs to be involved in something bigger than personal interests, and everyone needs to help others. In congregations I have served, I always thought and taught that commitment produced participation, and I still believe it does. But the opposite is also often true—commitment grows as people participate in the life of the church. It is one of the Church's most effective motivational tools. Compassion can be learned from sermons or books, but it is learned best by showing compassion. Pastoral care can be taught, but its glory and ecstasy are learned at deathbeds, in hospices, and in broken relationships.

**4. Devotion and service are two sides of the same spiritual coin.** Devotion and service call for a combination of the way Mary and Martha, sisters of Lazarus, looked at life. One wanted to keep close to Jesus for spiritual enrichment, and the other wanted to get the table ready to feed Him. In the work of God, both are needed—no leader's service can be truly divorced from his or her personal devotion to God. A balance between dwelling in quiet contact with Christ and going to do what He asks is the balance of Christianity. Effort without devotion leads to burnout, and devotion without effort results in lopsided other-worldliness.

**5. Service must be focused on what matters.** I gladly acknowledge that the idea that service must be focused on what matters comes from E. Stanley Jones, who insisted that when a church deals with marginal issues, it has little energy or time left for central issues. Jones recommends, "Take a fine-tooth comb and comb the account of the church at Antioch and you cannot find one single thing that was marginal, trivial, or not worthwhile. Everything that happened in Antioch had destiny in it. What happened there is vital and relevant for us today."[8]

**6. Happy Christians are active.** The converse is also true—active Christians are generally happy. Naturalist John Burroughs once observed, "I have discovered the secret of happiness—it is work, either with the hands or the head. The moment I have something to do, the draughts are open and my chimney draws, and I am happy."[9] Check out fulfilled Christians, and you find people who willingly work for great causes and invest large amounts of time and effort in Kingdom interests.

**7. Service keeps the power thirst in check.** Service in the name of Christ for some of the hurting of the world raises one's sensitivity to human need and makes any thirst for power seem unimportant. Service builds attentiveness to human want, and every Christian leader does himself or herself a favor by keeping close to persons in need.

**8. Service demands a high priority.** Jesus declared we were to "seek first the kingdom of God and His righteousness, and all these [other] things [would] be added" unto us (Matt. 6:33, NKJV). When Christ is given supremacy, meaning always increases in the rest of life. It is a principle of human existence that what we cherish must be first. A raided Detroit crack dealer had posted this statement on his office wall for his sales staff: "If you are planning on getting rich, you must forget about your girlfriends and family. . . . With hard work and dedication, we will all be rich in 12 months." I fear the drug dealer knew more about priorities than do many believers.

**9. Service connects me with the past and future of Christendom.** All Christians are beneficiaries of many persons who impacted them through Christian service in their past. Service is the Kingdom link with the past and the future. What we dream the future will be for our children and their children, we must craft for them now.

**10. Service must be focused on Christ.** Wendell Willkie once asked Franklin Roosevelt why he kept the sickly Harry Hopkins at his elbow. The president replied, "Through those doors flow an incessant stream of men and women who want something from me. Harry Hopkins, however, wants only to serve me. That's why he is always near me."[10] On a far nobler scale, Jesus also wants that from His disciples.

## THE INCREDIBLE POTENTIAL THAT SERVANTS POSSESS

For years I have been troubled and challenged and astounded by a powerfully penetrating paragraph from E. Stanley Jones written in 1970:

"In the church of the future the most important test of its power of survival and of its survival with power will be its capacity to win the two-thirds of its membership who are caught in the eddies of the inconsequential and marginal, and are going round and round, getting nowhere and producing little or nothing—except motion. This group is the greatest mission field in the church."[11] How can we marshal these human resources to revolutionize the world for Christ?

# 9

# Service—Seven Mysteries and Miracles

## *Eternal Results Can't Be Calculated Now*

Writers worry about words. That's why I fret about whether my meaning is clear when I use the words "mysteries" and "miracles" in the same context. Though those two words do not seem to belong together, they can't be separated in discussing serving Christ. So I am forced to hold the concepts of mysteries and miracles in my mind at the same time as I think and write about them. Though both holy mysteries and supernatural miracles are a great embarrassment to the secular mind, an awesome something permeates all that believers do in the name of Jesus.

Mystery deals with why God chooses flawed mortals like us to accomplish His work. The mystery side wonders how God accomplishes so much with so little, but He does. Mystery admits that benefits and blessings from serving others are difficult to describe, explain, or comprehend.

That mind-stretching word "miracle," as I use it here, refers to a supernatural enabling of our serving, so we never labor in our own strength. This also means that service done in Christ's name has some unexplainable present or future supernatural consequence. C. S. Lewis is right: "When we believe in miracles we embrace some reality beyond Nature."[1]

The miracle is this—the more we serve, the more meaning we enjoy in our relationship to Christ.

Serving in Jesus' name and for His sake produces its own rewards and satisfactions. Somewhere I read that missionary pioneer Hudson Taylor said miracles in Kingdom efforts have three stages—first, impossible; next, difficult; then, done. To be used of God to make the impossible happen is among the most exciting ways to spend one's lifetime. It gives us extravagant exhilaration to see God work miracles. Taylor's progression in service makes us want to sing Handel's "Hallelujah Chorus."

Let's consider several awe-inspiring mysteries and miracles of serving.

## MYSTERY/MIRACLE 1

### Service Makes Us Partners with Omnipotence

God uses us to fulfill the mission of Christ in an incredibly unequal partnership. Think of the risks He takes and the benefits we enjoy. In this partnership the Almighty is always the Senior Partner, and we are junior partners. The partnership showed in the early days of Christianity following the Resurrection—the disciples told everyone Jesus was alive, and that made all the difference in their lives. Ask Peter where Jesus was, and he would say, "He is here and everywhere we go, but working through us." Paul understood God to be his unseen Companion in every expression of his ministry, so he could say, "It is no longer I who live, but Christ lives in me" (Gal. 2:20, NKJV). It was David Livingstone and Jesus who went tramping together across Africa, planting gospel seed that continues to bear fruit to this day.

God, of course, has controlling interest in the partnership, but He allows the likes of us to assist Him in the task of transforming spiritually needy people and to be salt and light in the world. Scripture supports this partnership idea in a wide variety of ways. An example of what it can accomplish is heard by carefully considering Jesus' conversation with Philip.

You remember the tender though confusing event. As Jesus tried to console the disciples about His approaching death, Thomas asks with confused distress, "Lord, we don't know where you are going, so how can we know the way?" (John 14:5).

Then the Master assures him, "I am the way and the truth and the life. No one comes to the Father except through me" (v. 6).

Philip responds with uncertainty, "Show us the Father and that will be enough for us" (v. 8).

In His reply, Jesus gives the motivating force for all Christian service: "The person who trusts me will not only do what I'm doing but *even greater things,* because I, on my way to the Father, am giving you the same work to do that I've been doing. You can count on it" (John 14:12, TM, emphasis added).

*"Even greater things."* Just now I had to stop writing and walk around while I pondered the meaning and guarantee of those three words from our Master. Stand in awe as you count the potential of this intimate partnership with God. Think of the supernatural possibilities of this partnership—you are enabled to do God's work under God's direction for God's people with God's help, and you can count on God's results. The incredible outcome—"even greater things"!

Though you will always be the junior partner in relationship with Jesus, abundant divine resources are available to you. Our Senior Partner is always nearby for guidance, encouragement, and empowerment. Remember—being a junior partner with Christ is 10,000 times better than being senior partner with anyone else.

What magnificent possibilities are provided by this partnership. No wonder a young missionary who died early in the line of duty after having grown up in a wealthy, secular family, William Borden, could testify on the flyleaf of his Bible, "No reserves, no retreat, no regrets." His wholehearted commitment to a magnificent cause was his response to the faithfulness of his Partner.

We all need such a perspective and strength to keep on serving effectively and joyously. For some unexplainable, delightful reason, the Christian faith possesses this amazing paradox—God enables frail weaklings to do great work for Him instead of doing the work himself. But He provides the insight and the power. Our Senior Partner assigns us the most momentous task in the world and at the same time provides us with supernatural resources to accomplish it.

Pity those poor souls who try too little in the name of the living Lord or those who consider service to be some dutiful obligation they are forced to endure to gain God's favor. Both groups miss many satisfactions.

Martin Luther's observations about this holy partnership make us want to organize a march in the name of Jesus. He observed that Christians "are regarded by the world as fools, Cinderellas, as foot mats, as damned, impotent, and worthless people. But this does not matter. . . . I have seen many of these who, externally, tottered along very feebly, but when it came to the test and they faced the court, Christ bestirred Himself in them, and they became so staunch that the devil had to flee."[2]

Part of a prayer from Mother Teresa's helpers in Shishua Bhavan, Calcutta, clarifies this partnership issue for me: "Sweetest Lord, make me appreciative of the dignity of my high vocation and its many responsibilities. Never permit me to disgrace it by giving way to coldness, unkindness, or impatience. . . . Though you hid yourself behind the unattractive disguise of the irritable, the exacting, the unreasonable, may I still recognize you and say, 'Jesus, how sweet it is to serve you.'"[3]

## MYSTERY/MIRACLE 2

### Service Produces Satisfaction

Serving is a mystery and miracle that produces incredible interior development in us. If all human beings search for meaning, as I believe they do, then service to Christ is the best possible place to find ultimate fulfillment. I heard a pastor remark recently about service, "The promised land of satisfaction is just on the other side of your willing heart." When we wholeheartedly commit to a holy cause, the task often makes us noble and great as we do it.

The message of satisfaction in service shows in a story about two 10-year-old boys who lived a few miles from Springfield, Illinois. In October they offered to help an elderly neighbor rake leaves. After raking for two hours, one boy asked, "Mr. Kraft, are we playing or working? If this is working, I'm getting tired." The story teaches a lesson—we alone determine whether our service will be a joy or a burden to us. Serving can be fun.

• **Challenges apathy.** I am beginning to believe that much talk about apathy in contemporary churches may be rooted in a call to trivial service. Too many are asked to invest energy in meaningless busywork. Too many forget why or whom they serve. Too many seek prominence and prestige, finding it empty and unimportant. Too many, like Lazarus's sister Martha, have lost their focus so they are "fussing far too much and getting worked up over nothing" (Luke 10:41, TM). Of course, we can add spark and exhilaration to service by using words like creative, imaginative, life-changing, dynamic, energetic, stimulating, and challenging.

Lots of debate is going on now in the Church about why people do not want to give more time, energy, and imagination to the Church. The situation appears desperate. It is true that many youth groups do not have sponsors, Sunday School classes do not have teachers, and decision groups do not have enough people to decide. Apathy, laziness, and lack of commitment are loudly targeted as the reasons.

Seriously, could it be possible that apathy is actually rooted in seldom discussed issues like serving for wrong motives, devoting oneself to trifling ambitions, misusing God-given abilities, or ordering life by secondary priorities? It's a fixed law of service—satisfaction multiplies when motives are undiluted and self-sovereignty is given a knockout punch.

Satisfaction from service increases as we move closer to the Jesus lifestyle by relinquishing our craving for prominence, downplaying our guilt for not doing more, and quitting giving undue attention to what our image to others is. Simple, commonplace service like a cup of cold water, speaking comfort to the distressed, and serving the elderly packs an extraordinary wallop when done in Jesus' name. The unique, lasting satisfactions that service gives us come from doing what needs to be done for another in the powerful name of Jesus.

The issue about apathy must be faced in the Church: Is the cause worthy of time and energy? Is the cause important enough to challenge one's best? Is the goal Christ-centered? Few people are as turned on to paying for a church mortgage as they are to changing the world for Christ. Few people are as turned on to mowing the church lawn as they are to feeding the hungry of the world.

● **Magnetic causes.** Fulfillment derived from service increases as we involve ourselves in life-impacting causes. Look around—more, much more, waits to be accomplished in the name of Christ. In a world where science sends people to the moon, why can't we deliver housing for the homeless? In a time when the masses in the Western world are highly educated, why do we live under the dreadful abyss of war and the moral erosions that eat at the soul of society? In a time when countless people claim to be born again and religious causes fill stadiums, why is the human heart about like it has always been? The list of needed redemptive service keeps growing: people need the Lord, believers need to be discipled for Christ, reconciliation is needed between races, and better care for the elderly is needed.

● **Take risks.** Consider another factor that slows service. Some are afraid to welcome some needy person into their lives. It is a law of the Kingdom, like the law of gravity in the physical world, that love is risky. When faced with the risk, the line of reasoning sometimes says that those you serve might disappoint you, break your heart, use you, frustrate you, ruin your reputation. The possibilities are real, of course. But the other side must also be considered that says they may affirm you, return your love, give you fulfillment, or even change their community. They may help you see Jesus more clearly in the common tasks of your daily life. They may go where you will never go, to do what you will never be able to do.

• **Service satisfies.** You get hooked on the satisfactions of service the moment you accomplish something monumental for Christ. Then you can never be satisfied to go back to uninspiring trivial church work. Secular management authority Warren Bennis understands the idea well when he observes, "Human beings cannot live wholly or fully without giving themselves without reservation to something beyond themselves."[4] Many believers wait, without realizing it, to be genuinely challenged with possibilities and joys of service.

Christian essayist Frederick Buechner offers two convincing sentences that highlight this fulfillment issue: "By all the laws of logic and simple arithmetic, to give yourself away in love to another person would seem to mean that you end up with less of yourself left than you had to begin with. But the miracle is that just the reverse is true."[5] Serving stretches us to be more like Jesus, and that's the most satisfying experience of the human sojourn.

## MYSTERY/MIRACLE 3
### Service Cross-examines Our Usefulness

A song sung in many settings, including Martin Luther King Jr.'s funeral and United States President Bill Clinton's inaugural worship service at a Washington, D.C., African Methodist Episcopal Church on January 20, 1993, captures this idea in poetic language: "If I can help somebody as I pass along / . . . then my living shall not be in vain."

Too many think of the pew as a religious bleacher. Spectatorism has invaded the Church. The gospel has been taken out of the work clothes of ordinary people and put into the preacher's best Sunday clothes. Sadly, uselessness has become the standard practice for thousands of believers. Secular author Leo Rosten challenges uselessness: "I think the purpose of life is to be useful, to be responsible, to be compassionate. It is, above all, to matter: to count, to stand for something, to have made some difference that you lived at all."[6]

At first glance, uselessness appears to require nothing and produces no consequence—no action, no thought, and no accountability. But uselessness is a contradiction in terms for the Christian and is a serious issue to Jesus. Remember how Christ in the Good Samaritan passage chided those who did nothing as they went to the other side of the road? The idea continues in the story of Dives and Lazarus—the rich man was judged because he did nothing when he could have done so much. Strong condemnation was given the man who hid one talent in a napkin; he was called "a wicked, lazy servant" for doing nothing and was cast into "the darkness, where there will be weeping and gnashing of teeth" (Matt. 25:26, 30). In the parable of the soils (Mark 4:3-20), three soils were useless—one was hard, one was stony, and another was crowded. John the Baptist warns that useless chaff will be consumed (Matt. 3:12) and Christ says that useless weeds will be burned (Matt. 13:30). This common thread concerning uselessness, running through the teachings of the New Testament, should open the eyes of Christians everywhere.

Other examples of uselessness abound in Scripture. The priests in Jesus' time used their positions to squeeze ill-gotten gains from people; they were worse than useless. Rabbis sought chief places in public events. Levites hurried by to get ready for Temple sacrifices while ignoring the man who fell among robbers. The cold, calculating Pharisees, while wearing regulation clothes and often abusing others with their legalism, loaded unnecessary and useless burdens on those they led. Like a fire goes out without fuel and frequent stirring, spiritual devotion is often smothered by worn-out traditions; theoretical, no-meaning-to-life theology; and meaningless service.

Who wants to be judged by God as useless on the final day?

## MYSTERY/MIRACLE 4

### Service Inspires Christlike Action in Others

When I was about five years old, near the end of the Great Depression, a missionary came and asked our church and community to give financial support to his efforts for Christ. Stories he told about Africa thrilled my young mind. In our city, however, times were tough, and many people were on public assistance. Thus, the missionary's offering could not have been substantial. In that evening gathering, the missionary ambassador for Christ impacted me so much that to this day I never hear a missionary appeal without going back to that event so many years ago.

Why such an impact on me then and now? Because of the missionary's devotion. He said he gave by pulling his family's teeth when dental necessities required it and giving the money he saved by not going to a dentist to the cause. He reasoned, "Since native Africans pull their own teeth, why can't we?" And he did. Imagine how such an idea impressed a small boy who had a deathly fear of dentists.

That day my giving was motivated by a mental note that screamed in my inner world, "If the missionary could endure such pain to give an offering, why can't you empty your bank?" And I did. Christian service often does that, so our actions challenge others to become involved in the Kingdom. In fact, many followers of our Lord have never been motivated by the mission of Christ in the world—they are inactive because they don't see the point. Maybe they wait for someone to help them see the vision.

Modeling service, especially the costly, sacrificial kind, attracts others to service. Former United States President Jimmy Carter is a shining example with his involvement in Habitat for Humanity; many now participating in this housing effort for poor people never heard of the organization or considered the ministry possibilities of building houses until Carter became visible in this work.

One experienced pastor felt discouraged because he couldn't stimulate or inspire his congregation to try to accomplish great exploits for Christ. After a two-day vigil of prayer and fasting, he decided under divine direction that his service would be energetic and effective, even if he was forced to serve alone. The next Sunday he preached from Paul's idea to "follow my example, as I follow the example of Christ" (1 Cor. 11:1). He closed his sermon, which was mostly an autobiography of his spiritual pilgrimage, by reciting a covenant he had written during the two-day retreat. He read:

> ### My Service Covenant with Jesus
> • I will serve Christ constantly, consistently, and wholeheartedly.
> • I will not allow circumstances and excuses to sidetrack me.
> • I will obey God, no matter what others do.
> • I will show unconditional love to everyone.
> • I will serve God and others in both crises and calm.
> • I will do whatever is needed, no matter how lowly or lofty.

As you might expect, he never had to live out this covenant alone. Soon after his inspiring message, a groundswell of spiritual commitment to service started in his church. The next week in a leadership administrative meeting, one of the key leaders asked for the privilege of testifying about a new resolution to service. Others followed, and soon commitment from the leadership group splashed over the whole congregation. The change started when people saw how seriously devoted—maybe life or death seriously—their pastor was to do something useful for God and helpful to people. Christ-inspired service is contagious.

An old minister, one who carried years of sacrificial service on his shoulders and lots of mellowed love in his soul, remarked to a group of beginning pastors, "Boys and girls—be sure your ministry for Christ is good and important enough for your people to mimic and mirror, because that's what they do!"

That's a miracle and mystery of service—the people over time become what their leader is, especially in relationship to Christian service. Phenomenal Kingdom achievements are often accomplished by persons who have been infected with a holy contagion by some Christian who crossed their path while doing something great for God.

## MYSTERY/MIRACLE 5

### Service Outlasts Those Who Serve

I grew up in the days when most Christian families had

mottoes on the walls of their homes. For those from other places and other times, let me explain. A motto is a placard, sign, or plaque that states a Scripture verse or wise saying intended to point those who enter the home to God. Not always artistically produced, mottoes were apparently chosen more for message than for beauty. Sometimes a motto might be won at church for saying all the books of the Bible, for bringing five neighbors to Sunday School, or for spelling Bible names like Melchizedek correctly. We had a rather ugly-appearing motto in my childhood home that shouted, "Only one life, 'twill soon be past; / Only what's done for Christ will last." I remember the color, the lettering, the size, the shape, and who gave it to us. But I most remember the message.

That motto's impact lingers with me whenever I try to evaluate the priorities of my life. Many things have changed. The house has been gone for years, torn down to make room for an expanded airport. My grandparents who owned the home have been dead for more than 25 years. My father is in heaven. My mother is over 80. And I have grown children and grandchildren. But in spite of the changes of the years, the motto still haunts me in a positive way. I can't shake its message: Only what's done for Christ will last.

Last year following a class, two students waited until others left. Then they said something nice and frightening: "We love your stories about your ministerial heroes. It makes us feel as if we personally know the generation before us. But do you realize you will be remembered by us for the same reasons you remember them?"

My first reaction—"Wait a minute. That's too big a responsibility for me." Though my students' comments were humbling and terrifying, they are right about the powerful, long-term effect of influence. That's the reason I love to teach and write.

In a sermon called "A Promise for Life's Long Pull," Gardner Taylor went back to his alma mater, Oberlin College, to preach, where he exhorted graduates, faculty, and us about influence in Christian service: "I remember my days here with gratitude. The great names of those days have all disappeared. And you who teach here, how exercised you must be sometimes when it seems your students are determined not to learn. But mark, mark, mark me well. Long after you have quit this place, there will be men and women wearing upon themselves the weight of the years, who will look back upon you and thank God that you led them into the high disciplines of the faith."[7] Servants of Christ can count on the truth of those words; those they serve "will look back upon you and thank God that you led them into the high disciplines of the faith."

Christian service lasts beyond our lifetime and on into eternity. All Christian workers remember someone along their own journey who impacted them in ways they have never forgotten. Influence, in the lives of others we serve, is another mystery and miracle of service—God trusts and charges us with shaping new generations.

Service has no limits on talent, time, location, or outside control. Everyone can do something. You don't need anyone's permission to do something for God. Everyone can do something significant that outlasts his or her earthly existence. I'm counting on such beneficial fallout from my service—what's done for Christ lasts! I trust this certainty with my whole self—body, mind, soul, and will. And you can put your spiritual weight down on this promise too—"I tell you the truth, whatever you did for one of the least of these brothers of mine, you did for me" (Matt. 25:40).

## MYSTERY/MIRACLE 6

### Service Transforms Abstractions into Realities

Having spent most of my life in local congregations, with teacher colleagues in ministerial training settings, and among Christian writers, preachers, and publishers, I wonder if too much of contemporary Christianity doesn't have more talk than walk, more theory than practice, more image than substance.

Perhaps much of our present trouble comes from those who have unwittingly allowed or even intentionally encouraged the faith to become more rational than experiential, more conceptual than concrete, more abstract than active, more esoteric than life-changing. Apparently for some Christian pilgrims, the test of reason is a higher priority than spiritual development, and knowing about Christ is more important than knowing Christ. Though the Christian faith is not irrational, it doesn't have to pass every test that every doubter, adversary, or snob can dream up.

If my suspicions about overrationalizations are even close to accurate, changes must be made. Christianity must again become a way of life purchased, if need be, with our own energy and blood. Acts of service must turn our abstract notions into care for the sick, bread for the hungry, and training for the young.

For that to happen, deliberate action is needed to take Christ to the cutting edge of modernity, where He belongs. I have bold, radical service in mind that takes Christianity to the front lines of society, such as AIDS patients in hospitals, mixed-up youth in menacing ghettos, dying sufferers in hospices, hopeless prisoners in crowded jails, pregnant unmarried frightened girls in cities and suburbs, throwaway children in forsaken places, and up-and-outers and down-and-outers everywhere. It means taking Christ to present day Mars Hill settings like secularized educational institutions and to the influential halls of government. Max De Pree, insightful author on leadership issues, is right: "We cannot become what we need to be by remaining what we are."[8] Let's become like the Master so we take Christ to every setting He would go to if He walked the earth in human form in our times.

Christ's call to a revitalized faith glistens in the following paragraph about Dietrich Bonhoeffer's commitments for Christ, written by pediatrician and child psychiatrist Robert Coles. Coles is a researcher on the spiritual lives of children and one who regularly teaches an undergraduate course at Harvard titled The Literature of Christian Reflection. Coles made this observation:

> He [Bonhoeffer] proceeded in a quiet yet determined manner to live out his ideas. Put differently, he had no in-

terest in moral analysis or moral rhetoric unconnected to the possibilities and predicaments of a given life. He seemed intent on really testing his own ideas: how persuasive were they with respect to *his* actions—never mind those of others? He worried, I suppose it can be said, about "cheap grace" afforded intellectuals, self-appointed moralists, preachers, ideologues of various persuasions—who tell others what is good and bad, what and what not to do, and yet manage to escape the pain or sacrifice entailed in all sorts of ethically demanding trials.[9]

I propose that we spiritually re-energize every act of service so we become radically Christian in every part of our pilgrimage. I propose that we share Christ interestingly and intentionally. I propose we go all out—heart and soul—to help persons who need us. I propose we become stubbornly resolute to bring about a no-nonsense spiritual renaissance to our society. I propose we challenge all the destructive myths like "I've done my share," "I'm too old," "I'm not trained," "No one needs me," and "No one asked me."

The following story happened during the United States civil rights cyclone. Tessie, a schoolgirl who helped desegregate McDonogh 19 School in New Orleans, was told by her maternal grandmother, Martha, "You see, my child, you have to help the good Lord with His world! He put us here—and He calls us to help Him out."[10] That's our call too—to help God with His world. To do that we must do an end run around every hindrance.

## Mystery/Miracle 7

### Service Shapes Me Forever

Some experiences change us forever. Sometimes efforts impact us so significantly because they involve us in meeting a critical need for someone. Or they may be done in an area of life where we have never been before. Examples in my life include a mission trip to a third world country, holding a dying patient's hand as he changed worlds, and as a 10-year-old, helping an intoxicated neighbor find his way home.

One of Coles's descriptions helps me see how service experiences uniquely shape my life. He believes satisfying service is "lives called into action in different ways and for various reasons and for varying lengths of time."[11] To make his idea sizzle in my life of service, I need to edit Coles slightly to make him say, "lives called into action *for Christ and my fellow human beings* in different ways and for various reasons and for varying lengths of time."

A striking historical example of the shaping power of an event is the idealistic young people who participated in the civil rights freedom march on Washington. Those times are gone, and our memories of the events have dimmed over the years. The crowd returned to their jobs, Martin Luther King Jr. was murdered, and marchers went home to take up their lives. But the impact continues through the lives of those who were there. And the world was changed forever. Like salt in the teachings of Jesus, those marchers have grown older and taken places of influential service all over America. They now strive for justice in schools, colleges, financial institutions, churches, law offices, centers of power, and seats of government. Their service continues for years after the events.

They still work for the cause, and the cause enriches them. They have done what the institution would allow them to do. They have experienced what medical doctor Helen De Rosis suggests about the worth of service: "Put yourself wholeheartedly into something, and energy grows. If, on the other hand, you are divided and conflicted about what you are doing, you create anxiety. And the amount of physical and emotional energy consumed by anxiety is exorbitant."[12] Think how useful Dr. De Rosis's concept is for your corner of the Kingdom.

## NEVER STOP—KEEP SERVING

Why keep serving? Why keep trying? Why serve when it seems that you no longer make much difference? Paul gives his reason: "The love of Christ constraineth us" (2 Cor. 5:14, KJV). That's my reason too. To put it in a more earthy way, consider the slogan I saw on a ragged T-shirt in London's Heathrow Airport:

Your team can make you hustle . . .
Your coach can put you on the team . . .
A scout can give you a scholarship . . .
But only you can make you a player.

Devotional writer Oswald Chambers makes me want to pray with his summary: "Paul says he is gripped by the love of God, that is why he acts as he does. Men may call him mad or sober, but he does not care; there is only one thing he is living for, and that is to persuade men of the judgment seat of God and the love of Christ. This abandon to the love of Christ is the one thing that bears fruit in life."[13]

Later in the same book, Chambers rounds out the idea: "If I am devoted to the cause of humanity only, I will soon be exhausted and come to the place where my love will falter; but if I love Jesus Christ personally and passionately, I can serve humanity though I am treated as a door-mat."[14]

There you have it. Why serve? Why keep going? Why refuse to give up? *The love of Christ constraineth us*—that's why! And we must keep remembering: "This abandon to the love of Christ is the one thing that bears fruit in life."

# 10

# Mission—
# Fuel for Vision

## Unleashing Christ's Magnetic Purpose

"Christ's mission recharges our batteries rather than draining them. Burnout is rooted in unclear mission." These words from a keynote address touched a sensitive nerve for conferees. A buzz of conversation followed at the end of the session.

Let's move the speaker's idea closer to us. Though few church leaders would disagree that contemporary Christianity has its mission blurred, many of us would not think of ourselves as being affected by this problem. But we are. Just as the speaker's sentences prodded conference participants to reconsider their part in mission, his words do the same to us.

Somewhere in our past, we encountered Christ's almost irresistible attractiveness. So we know from personal experience that mission draws people to Christ and that mission is an alarming missing ingredient in many contemporary congregations.

Jesus predicted His death and promised His cross would provide an amazing attraction: "And I, as I am lifted up from the earth, will attract everyone to me and gather them around me" (John 12:32, TM). I can't read the passage without stopping to catch my spiritual breath. It reminds us in no uncertain terms that our Lord Christ is the major attraction of the Church in every generation and culture.

Concerning this glorious incongruity, New Testament scholar William Barclay commented, "The whole lesson of history is that Jesus was right. It was on the magnet of the Cross that Jesus pinned His hopes. And Jesus was right because love lives long after might and power and force is dead. . . . Empires founded on force have vanished, leaving only a memory, which with the years become even fainter. But the empire of Christ, founded upon a Cross, each year extends its sway. . . . The Prince of Love on the Cross is a king who has His throne for ever in the hearts of men."[1]

## HE PROMISED, "I . . . WILL DRAW," AND HE DOES

Mission now stands at the heart of the gospel as it has for nearly 2,000 years. Jesus promised, "I . . . will draw" (v. 32), and He does. His mission keeps inspiring individuals to give themselves to His cause. And we commit ourselves gladly.

Two significant questions must be considered: Who can calculate the impact that mission has created across church history? Who can envision what renewed mission might do for us? But even while wrestling with those questions, we must remember a timeless truth—the Christ of the center cross has an incredible magnetism that draws people to himself. The Cross, contrary to what might be expected, attracts instead of turning people off.

Our dilemma, then, as Christ's spokespersons is to lift up Jesus with all His life-changing demands in a time when our society seems given to self-seeking individualism and acquisition of more possessions. We think they'll reject Him. But lots of secularists apparently have never really heard the challenge of Christ's mission, nor have they heard about the high quality of life our Lord offers. If they knew more about Christ and saw more of His way of life in us, they might fall in love with Him as we have.

The Lord Christ has many ways of capturing people's affections and summoning them to come and die for His cause. The same radical message that drew us to the Savior will draw others. I experienced that attraction all over again

when I read about Him in the December 1994 issue of *Life:*
"In only three years Jesus defined a mission and formed
strategies to carry it out. With a staff of 12 unlikely men, He
organized Christianity, which today has branches in all the
world's countries and a 32.4-percent share of the world's
population, twice as big as its nearest rival."[2] It's true—the
mission of Christ, even as it attracted the original Twelve and
us, keeps drawing others wherever it is shared in love with
power.

For servants of Christ, His mission means living out the
divine purpose. Mission visionaries, not satisfied to be
hirelings, live out mission and take Christ into their daily
lives.

A similar challenge in the secular arena shows in a story
about United States President Franklin D. Roosevelt. It is reported the president sat waiting for an acceptance from
Joseph Davies to become the United States ambassador to
Russia. Impressed by Roosevelt's lofty arguments for ap-
pointing him, Davies remarked, "Mr. President, it seems to
me that you are giving me a big job."

Roosevelt countered quickly, "I am giving you a mission—not a job."

That's what Christ does for us—He provides His servants with an incredible mission, bigger than all the com-
bined jobs in the world. And His servants willingly pay any
price that love requires.

Our Lord's mission unleashes opportunities for us to
participate in a cause that requires our best energy and captures our most creative imagination. Such a commitment to
His mission motivates our efforts, purifies our intentions,
and refocuses our values.

Our Lord's love moves us to noble gratitude, so we
wholeheartedly embrace John's admonition: "By this we
know love, because He laid down His life for us. And we also ought to lay down our lives for the brethren" (1 John 3:16,
NKJV).

The same amazing attraction of Christ's mission inspired David Livingstone to write near the end of his long

missionary ministry in Africa, "Christ is the greatest Master I have ever known. . . . Jesus Christ is the only Master supremely worth serving. He is the only ideal that never loses His inspiration. . . . We go forth in His name, in His power, in His Spirit, to serve Him."[3] Theologian Emil Brunner observed, "The church exists by mission as fire exists by burning."

## THE INTERPLAY BETWEEN MISSION AND VISION

In my customary practice before beginning a book manuscript, I do scribble writing for months before I start writing for others to read. About this chapter I wrote myself a note: "Write about the connection of vision and mission. A vision fires mission! Or does mission fire vision? I am having trouble making up my mind." I still am.

Students tell me I inadvertently use "mission" and "vision" interchangeably in classes on Christian leadership, and when they ask which word I mean, I frequently respond, "I'm not sure." I am not completely sure whether mission or vision comes first. Both are significant and needed in Kingdom efforts.

This much I know: mission informs and inspires vision. Christ's mission remains constant across calendars, cultures, generations, and geographies. But to activate mission in a specific setting requires vision. Mission is *why*; vision is *how*.

### The Meaning of Mission

Mission deals with purpose and determines what business the Church is really in. Jesus summarized it in two mission statements: (1) "All authority in heaven and on earth has been given to me. Therefore go and make disciples of all nations, baptizing them in the name of the Father and of the Son and of the Holy Spirit, and teaching them to obey everything I have commanded you. And surely I am with you always, to the very end of the age" (Matt. 28:18-20); (2) "You will be my witnesses in Jerusalem, and in all Judea and Samaria, and to the ends of the earth" (Acts 1:8). The ingredients of our Lord's mission, crystal clear in these two passages, appear often throughout the Gospels and in Acts. Mission provides direction, purpose, and rationale for what the Church is and does.

Mission also provides a motivational engine that drives ministry. Mission clarifies the Church's reason for being, defines its arena for action, and tests its various ministries. It calls us to authentically follow the mind of Christ in all dimensions of our personal and congregational efforts.

### Activating Mission

Mission is the raw material of vision. Vision needs constant commitment to mission and must always deal with how mission is implemented in a specific way in a particular setting or assignment. Vision requires discovering a perspective of what God wants done and then designing strategies to fulfill the Father's plan.

Vision demands clarity of purpose. Vision requires constant connection to Christ and Scripture so you can see possibilities for mission achievement in every setting. Visionary servants of Christ accomplish mission partly because of what they see and partly because of what they refuse to see. Vision helps us realize that Kingdom service is the most satisfying way to live.

Not any vision will do, however. What we need is a vision that connects every expression of service to mission. The vision we need commits us to what really matters to Christ. Christian leaders can communicate a vision of mission in various ways: (1) frequent preaching with biblical authority, (2) person-to-person conversation, (3) administrative leadership, (4) commitment to the cause, and (5) example.

Delightful adventure comes as we succeed in accomplishing Christ's mission in our lives, in the Church, and in the world. What could be more fulfilling than being involved in such a magnificent, supernatural, and eternal cause?

Implementing mission takes our best effort coupled with supernatural resourcing from God. Willis Harman, scientist, futurist, and president of the Institute of Noetic Sciences, explains how implementing mission works in secular business activity: "Once the vision is created and there is commitment to it, factors and forces to bring about its realization are already set in motion. 'Coincidences,' 'lucky breaks,' and 'following hunches' are likely to play a part; but actualization of the vision comes about in ways that feel mysteriously like something more than planned steps plus chance events."[4]

The Church, however, views this process somewhat differently. To unleash the impact of mission in our efforts for Christ, what Harman considers "chance events" we believe to be divine guidance and supernatural empowerment. We believe the God who leads is significantly more dependable than coincidences, lucky breaks, or following hunches.

Let's explore the benefits of a clearly communicated, biblically based mission to shape and nourish all our efforts for Christ.

## BENEFIT 1

### A Vision of Mission Centers a Church on Christ

Some church futurist is reported to have said that baby boomers will commit to a cause or person but not to an organization or idea. This same observation could be made for many age-groups. A pivotal reality is built into the fabric of Christ's teachings; He never intended His mission to be centered on concepts or institutions. A Person—Jesus, Lord and Master—is the attractive magnet of His mission. The attraction He offers is the opportunity of knowing Him intimately and finding a delightful Christ-quality life.

Such a new life attracts broken, dysfunctional, confused, frustrated, sinful people. And mission calls us to communicate these realities in ways they can understand.

But how? Often by helping a decision group or congregation in forming a mission statement, a leader takes the group back to Christ. Serious discussions of the mission of any church invariably takes the group back to Scripture, and Scripture takes us to Christ. Logically, emotionally, and volitionally, the Lord Jesus must be the Foundation of all the Church does.

One reason churches lose their drawing power is because they commit themselves to many good things while neglecting the main thing. Trying to justify their existence to their community or constituency, they have neglected who they are supposed to be, what they are supposed to do, and who they are called to serve.

## BENEFIT 2

### A Vision of Mission Clarifies a Church's Purpose

If Christ calls a person to come and die so that he or she may really live, then it follows that His Church must also be ready to die for Him. Too often in the present scheme of things, the Church is viewed by outsiders and some insiders as an institution that protects itself at any cost. If this perspective is accurate, it presents a contradiction of the essential nature of the Church.

Doesn't the Church's mission start with Friday's darkness so she can enjoy Sunday's victory? The Church's mission, then, compels her to give herself poor, to die for resurrection, and to win the world at any cost. Those demands sound like bitter medicine, or should I say strong poison, to those who see the Church as localized on the corner of Main and First Street or those who view the Church as a nice setting where the genteel gather occasionally to receive comfort for facing a stress-producing work environment.

Others think institutional survival is the main goal. Survival cannot be the Church's most pressing concern. Her buildings, personnel, and prominence are significant only as they relate to her mission. An old Scottish preacher was exactly right when he observed, "The church is on her last legs. She has always been on her last legs—that's when she does her best work."

Fulfilling Christ's mission provides the Church with her most authentic credentials and her most vigorous energizing force. Certainly most of us are more attracted to a church that risks dying at the cutting edge of contemporary society than dying from old age brought on by inconsequential triviality.

It's time to put the debate aside about choosing salvation or social service. The Church must do both for the right reasons. While the Church has many acceptable strategies and a picnic basket full of programs, its main mission is summarized in John Wesley's mandate: "You have nothing to do but save souls. Therefore, spend and be spent in the work." Our Lord calls the Church to be agents of spiritual transformation in people's lives. Every program, ministry, and dollar must be directed to that cause.

An understanding of mission calls every church to stop dabbling in everything from politics to real estate. Mission clarifies the Church's unique task—to do what Francis Asbury admonished: "Offer them Christ." Perhaps contemporary society misreads the Church, or perhaps the Church misspeaks herself, but many secularists have never really heard the good news of Christ. That's why they don't see the point of why the Church is significant.

To keep its purpose clear, the Church must use the mission of Christ to shape her budgeting, calendaring, spending, preaching, building, programming, and relationships. The masses think we are committed to survival, and many churches are. That has to change, and priorities have to be refocused. The time is past due to use Christ's mission to clarify the Church's reason for being.

Mission calls us to stop all useless compromises that homogenize biblical and ethical issues into a confusing nonstandard for living or for the Church. The clouded mission has to be made clear so persons in the pews do not think the church is a place to make them comfortable, to set the government straight about its policies, to spout off about the latest theological fad, to make social service take priority over spiritual transformation, or where reason sits in judgment on faith. Mission calls us to refocus on the basic essentials of the gospel so we effectively wrestle with the issues of our day by applying the teachings of Scripture to our times.

For a church to resist contemporary application of mission makes us victims of the irony that is so visible in so many places. When the church commits to survival, it finally dies or shrivels up into nothingness. On the contrary, the church that reaches to fulfill Christ's mission in the world prospers. Most churches are committed to maintaining themselves and to providing activity for their people. Many are in a survival mode because they are busy without results. Some are even controlled by a strong leader (lay or clergy) but are not achieving anything. But control, activity, and maintenance do not a true church make. The church must have some measurable achievement that fulfills its mission if it is to please the Lord and attract people.

## BENEFIT 3

### A Vision of Mission Generates Resources

Great causes inspire people to give their creativity, energy, money, and stamina. Present-day examples of how great causes draw resources can be observed in the work of Chuck Colson, Promise Keepers, and Compassion International.

By "resources" I mean money, but I also mean more than money. Since money is distilled effort, it can most helpfully be viewed as the people giving of themselves. It's true, isn't it, that when individuals give money, they are actually giving time, sweat, and energy to the cause of Christ? Thus, effort and money should be equally cherished as flowing from the same worthy motivation that mission stimulates.

Consider the competence issue too. Doing a great work for God encourages a person and group to give their best effort. We reason, "I must do this work well, because I'm doing it for God." I remember receiving beyond-the-call-of-duty help from a supervising nun in a Catholic hospital who remarked after I thanked her, "I'm doing this for you and for the Father too." Mission does that when it challenges every believer to give his or her best. As the workman digging a hole as part of a cathedral project told the one querying him, "I'm building this sanctuary for the glory of God, and that means it has to be my best."

Mission provides a magnet for commitment and money. The founder of the China Inland Mission (now Overseas Missionary Fellowship), Hudson Taylor, discovered and lived by his three-level concept: "God's work, done in God's way, will never lack God's supply." This mission magnet has worked for thousands of other Kingdom efforts, including George Mueller with his orphanages in England and Amy Car-michael with her work among children in South India.[5] Support and commitments increase when people understand how mission can be achieved and how their efforts fit into the overall scheme of what God is doing.

At the same time, mission judges efforts, decisions, and traditions. Like a laser beam, it detects efforts that no longer contribute to achieving mission. It helps question practices rooted in habitual but ineffective methods, customs, and practices. One observer accurately remarked, "Anytime the Church does something more than once, it likely becomes a tradition." This evaluation spin-off of mission can be very useful, because every church has at least one obsolete activity or practice that should be scrapped. Continuing dialogue concerning mission tends to eliminate such programs over time and releases energy and resources for front-line expression of Christian mission in our time.

Here's how mission generates resources—a vision of mission stimulates involvement, excites giving, and produces an accumulation of energy and resolve. Churches plagued with apathy and low involvement should try evaluating their efforts against the magnetic mission of the Master.

## BENEFIT 4

### A Vision of Mission Prioritizes Strategies

A vision of mission serves as a road map for a congregation. Direction for ministry most often comes from understanding the essential task of the church. Thus, mission is more than something to do. Rather, it is the rudimentary driving force rooted in the nature of the church.

In prioritizing strategies, the busyness trap must be avoided. A congregation never accomplishes mission simply because everyone keeps busy. Likewise, an overly scheduled Christian worker may not do much to achieve mission. It is easy for a congregation to become too busy; sometimes this occurs to insiders who have no time to consider which should take place in and through the church. Outsiders sometimes see it immediately and wonder how the work of the church is different from that of other community organizations.

Certainly activity is needed, but it must have a clearly understood purpose. Fulfilling mission starts with an understanding of Christ's purpose for your church and then designing activities to accomplish that mission. It requires activity for a reason.

A clearly communicated sense of mission prioritizes the work of God because it helps participants see what needs to be done and what they can do. Understanding mission helps a congregation see the big picture of what God is doing and develops a wider perspective among leaders. Ideally, such a perspective deals with the real stuff of life—the good, the bad, the problems, and the solutions. Then a clearer focus on mission makes ministry more understandable, so it helps break down resistance to the layperson's commonly held viewpoint that the pastor tries to keep him or her busy doing good but nonessential things.

A clear vision of mission helps us see that new strategies are often needed for new times. While the mission of Christ remains the same over time, the methods for accomplishing His mission change. Sadly, churches splinter more over new methods than over doctrinal, personnel, or money issues. For some confusing reason, methods almost become sacred cows, so we forget that the most entrenched present-day methods were once controversial new strategies.

Every old method, every new ministry, every innovative ministry, and every established tradition should be continually evaluated against the mission of Christ for His Church. Frequent or even continuous talk about mission in a congregation creates a climate in which these questions are naturally asked: "Is this ministry or activity accomplishing its intended purpose? If the answer is yes, what does it accomplish? If the answer is no, what should be done about it?"

Be quick to activate the new when it serves mission. Bury the old when it no longer achieves mission. But don't begin the novel or bury the old for the exercise of being different just to be different.

## BENEFIT 5

### A Vision of Mission Makes Good on Kingdom Promises

Coming to Christ provides a top-quality life now and hope of heaven. Our Lord promises new lives for old. He offers forgiveness of sin, relationship with God, church friendships, helps for marriage and parenting, plus enablement to face every dimension of living.

Let's admit, however, that faithful attenders sometimes experience something much different at church. Too frequently they encounter cranky members, dysfunctional acquaintances, harpy preaching, closed cliques, out-of-touch worship practices, and reprimands demanding more prayer, more giving, and more work. You have the picture from experience.

Looking for answers, they find questions. Looking for solutions, they find problems. Looking for explanations, they find confusion. Looking for wholeness, they find fragmentation. Somehow promise and reality are out of sync.

Promises will be fulfilled more often when we see to it that a constant calibrating to mission is being done throughout the congregation. This can be achieved by asking: How does our ministry look to Christ? What would He change in our church if He were present in human form? What promises does He want kept that are now being ignored or compromised? A clear sense of mission clarifies and empowers the promises a church makes to people.

## BENEFIT 6

### A Vision of Mission Undermines Rationalizations

The decision group at the church comes to order for its monthly meeting. The church's attendance and influence has not been dazzling. Three families have moved to a church down the street, two families have taken job transfers this month, and the key lay leader wants to take a year off so he can have more time for recreation on weekends.

But Pastor Cliff gives a spin doctor presentation that would make any politician proud. His words ring with assurance: "We are in a winter stage when things look bleak but spring always follows winter. We are thinking about having a real estate agent scout out possibilities for relocating in two to three years. We are discussing the possibilities of impacting our whole city for Christ. Offerings are down, but that should be expected at this time of year. By 12 months from now, we should be ready to remodel the rest rooms and recarpet the sanctuary. And there is some discussion among the moneyed people in the church about buying a snowplow for the church to use next winter." Note the fluff and missing specifics. Most of the members of the decision group smile like pacified babies, and everything goes on as usual.

Many good people are experts at fooling themselves into thinking things are better than they are. Spin doctoring, so common in business and politics, has invaded the Church. It almost elevates an excuse to the equivalent of effective action. Excuses are counterfeit reasons we give to explain why we should not be expected to live up to the demands of mission in the church. Sometimes the spin doctoring takes almost as much effort as genuine achievement would.

Excuses and rationalizations usually work pretty well because no one wants the negative consequences of facing the facts. No one likes to answer why the church is not more effective. No one likes to consider tough questions about why we can't impact more people with the gospel. No one likes to push committees to do what they agreed to do. No one likes to try to motivate others to do something they are not willing to do themselves.

But eventually excuses catch up with us in the church— after years of fooling ourselves, the church may be going precisely nowhere and doing precisely nothing. We may have kept the doors open, but nothing happens when we come in. On the contrary, true vision of mission keeps us from settling for mediocrity and passing it off as praiseworthy.

Christ's mission gives a standard a church can use to evaluate and modify its work. Fulfilling Christ's mission means the church wins more people. Fulfilling Christ's mission means the church disciples more people into spiritual maturity. Fulfilling Christ's mission means the church impacts its community for Christ. Fulfilling Christ's mission means the church tries to touch every strata of society.

As we have seen, mission, properly used, provides the church with a self-administered evaluation system. Like a physical exam in the physician's office, the church's vital signs are checked against accepted norms to see if it is healthy and well. Then lifestyles change; medications and even corrective surgeries are recommended for good health. That's what mission can do for the church.

The Father wants His Church vigorous, robust, and aggressive in impacting its world. Mission gives us a divinely sanctioned criterion for evaluation—if we will use it.

The following four simple steps can help you evaluate whether the mission of Christ is being fulfilled in you and your church: (1) Judge your service by results rather than intentions, (2) be honest in your self-talk about spiritual achievement, (3) try seeing your church as Christ sees it, and (4) resist shortcuts, because they seldom work or satisfy.

## TEN CHARACTERISTICS OF A DYNAMITE MISSION STATEMENT

Before developing a mission statement, it may be useful to consider what qualities such a statement should have. Try these on for size:

1. Mission starts with a group encounter with God.
2. Mission determines priorities and judges activities.
3. Mission aligns words, emotions, and actions.
4. Mission discourages dealing with secondary issues.
5. Mission shapes a church's future.
6. Mission is worthy of everyone's full support.
7. Mission should be rooted in reality.
8. Mission is an expression of serious intent.
9. Mission expresses a church's unique role in culture.
10. Mission helps a congregation see ministry as it can be.

## UNLEASHING MISSION IN YOUR CHURCH

I am coming to believe more and more that a congregation isn't helped much by more esoteric or theoretical discussion about vision and mission. But any church can be greatly inspired in their service to Christ by using some simple process that allows people time to ponder and pray about what God wants in their church. They need time to think together about what He wants to do through them in their particular setting at this time. Since the process seems more important than the strategy, design the session any way that seems most useful to your group.

The message of this chapter, however, is to find useful ways to allow the same mission that drives your ministry to impact those who serve with you. You may want to build these concepts into your process:

**1. Prayer.** Start with prayer for implementing mission. Use any prayer pattern that seems useful, but try to focus on the meaning of vision and mission for your situation.

**2. Perspective.** Check out the Jesus perspective. Prepare handouts and discuss scripture that helps your group understand the purpose of Jesus for the Church and the world. How does your church and its ministry look to Christ? What would He say if He were sitting in physical form at the head of the table in your decision group?

**3. Discussion.** Give time for people to think and discuss. Most laypersons have not been involved in a discussion of mission. Generally they have been told what the mission of Christ was and then diplomatically shamed for not accomplishing it.

**4. Writing.** Ask them to write what they think mission is. Assure them that you do not plan to collect the responses, but writing often increases the focus of good ideas.

**5. Dreaming.** Urge them to think bigger than they have ever thought before. A wonderfully effective church leader I know urges people to "go out on the limb, because that's where the best fruit can always be found."

**6. Being specific.** Ask them to be specific. Somewhere in the process of pondering mission for your church, it becomes necessary to make specific plans and proposals. Disallow speeches about limited resources and opportunities, and give high visibility to potential and possibility.

**7. Identification of obstacles.** Identify obstacles that hold your church back from achieving mission. Try steering the conversation away from negative carping, and try to clearly identify specific hindrances that can be changed with a little effort. Start with the small ones first.

**8. Looking to the future.** Encourage them to accept responsibility for making the future as bright as God wants it to be in your church. We are the pacesetters the next generation will discuss 50 years from now.

## THE CHALLENGE—APPLY MISSION TO THESE TIMES

Our entire society, including our churches, reels from the incredible changes and destructive trends we see everywhere. Living near the turn of the new century can be more than a bit overwhelming. But in spite of these times, or because of them, we are called to achieve Christ's mission in His Church and in His world. Let's view our opportunities as a blend of challenges and opportunities.

I was deeply moved by Tom Sine's call to mission in *Wild Hope:* "If we don't begin in our lives, professions and churches to anticipate both the new challenges and new opportunities the twenty-first century brings us, we will quite literally be buried alive in the onrushing avalanche of change. No longer can we drive headlong into the future with our eyes fixed on our rear-view mirrors. We must learn to take the future seriously in every arena of life."[6]

As a wholehearted response to the challenge, why not affirm that the Christ whose mission we seek to fulfill has the game plan for our time, accurate understanding of our situation, and power to turn our contemporary world around? The Christ of mission allows us the privilege of being architects of the enduring.

# NOTES

## Chapter 1

1. *Skyview Magazine,* July 1995, 37.
2. "Points to Ponder," *Reader's Digest,* March 1991, 161.
3. Darrell Jodock, "Called to Change," *Christian Century,* January 25, 1995, 81.
4. Paul Scherer, "Hath God Indeed Said?" in *20 Centuries of Great Preaching* (Waco, Tex.: Word, 1971), 10:318.
5. Dan Wakefield, "In Search of Miracles," as quoted in "Are We Living in the New Age of Miracles?" *Current Thoughts and Trends* 11, No. 7 (July 1995): 7.
6. J. I. Packer, "The Holy Spirit: God at Work," *Christianity Today,* March 19, 1990, 29.
7. Herbert Lockyer, *All the Miracles of the Bible* (Grand Rapids: Zondervan Publishing House, 1961), 15.
8. Bill Bright, "Supernaturally Commissioned," *Current Thoughts and Trends* 10, No. 12 (December 1994): 8-9.

## Chapter 2

1. A. Skevington Wood, *Life by the Spirit* (Grand Rapids: Zondervan Publishing House, 1963), 48.
2. Wayne Oates, *The Presence of God in Counseling* (Waco, Tex.: Word, 1986), 99.
3. Albert E. Day, *The Captivating Presence* (Nashville: Parthenon Press, 1971), 6.
4. Fulton J. Sheen, *On Being Human* (Garden City, N.Y.: Image, 1983), 191.
5. Leonard Griffith, *The Eternal Legacy from the Upper Room* (San Francisco: Harper and Row, 1963), 94.
6. Reuben P. Job and Norman Shawchuck, *A Guide to Prayer for Ministers and Other Servants* (Nashville: Upper Room, 1983), 101.
7. "Author Warns Church Leaders," *Colorado Springs Gazette Telegraph,* August 19, 1992, B2.
8. Oates, *Presence of God in Counseling,* 120.
9. Browne Barr, "Ministry as Midwifery," *Christian Century,* June 27—July 4, 1990, 625.
10. Charles S. Denison, "Soulwork," *Leadership,* spring 1992, 105.
11. Thomas Kelly, *A Testament of Devotion,* in Denison, "Soulwork," 105.
12. Job and Shawchuck, *Guide to Prayer,* 101.
13. A. W. Tozer, *The Pursuit of God* (Harrisburg, Pa.: Christian Publications, 1948), 8.
14. Ibid., 9.
15. Ralph Spaulding Cushman, *Hilltop Verses and Prayers* (Nashville: Abingdon-Cokesbury Press, 1945), 74.
16. Paraphrase of Psalm 13 in Stephen Mitchell, *A Book of Psalms* (New York: HarperCollins, 1993), 6.
17. Thomas Oden, *Requiem* (Nashville: Abingdon Press, 1995), 123.
18. Judith C. Lechman, *The Spirituality of Gentleness* (San Francisco: Harper and Row, 1987), 46.
19. Dag Hammarskjöld, *Markings* (New York: Knopf, 1964), 50.

20. Tony Campolo, *The Power Delusion* (Wheaton, Ill.: Victor Books, 1983), 163.

21. Day, *Captivating Presence*, 15.

22. Maxie D. Dunnam, *Alive in Christ* (Nashville: Abingdon Press, 1982), 54.

23. Job and Shawchuck, *Guide to Prayer*, 33.

## Chapter 3

1. Tony Sargent, *The Sacred Anointing* (Wheaton, Ill.: Crossway Books, 1994), 57.

2. James Forbes, *The Holy Spirit and Preaching* (Nashville: Abingdon Press, 1989), 49.

3. G. Campbell Morgan, *Preaching* (New York: Revell, 1937), 36.

4. Charles Spurgeon, *Lectures to My Students* (London: Marshall, Morgan and Scott, 1954), 189.

5. Sargent, *Sacred Anointing*, back cover.

6. E. M. Bounds, *The Preacher and Prayer* (Kansas City: Nazarene Publishing House, 1963), 73.

7. Dennis Kinlaw, *Preaching in Demonstration of the Spirit and Power* (Philadelphia: Fortress Press, 1988), 41.

8. J. Daniel Baumann, *An Introduction to Contemporary Preaching* (Grand Rapids: Baker Book House, 1972), 285.

9. Richard Busch, "A Strange Silence," *Christian Century*, March 22, 1995, 316.

10. Morgan, *Preaching*, 37.

11. Brief quotation in *Current Thoughts and Trends* 11, No. 6 (June 1995): 21.

12. Ibid., 19.

13. Kinlaw, *Spirit and Power*, 41.

14. Ibid., 11.

15. Ibid., 12.

16. Gardner C. Taylor, *How Shall They Preach?* (Elgin, Ill.: Progressive Baptist Publishing House, 1977), 27.

17. William Still, "The Holy Spirit in Preaching," *Christianity Today*, September 2, 1957, 9.

18. Kinlaw, *Spirit and Power*, 15.

19. David H. C. Read, "Eutychus—or the Perils of Preaching," *Princeton Seminary Bulletin*, n.d., 170.

20. Andrew Blackwood, *Preaching from the Bible* (Nashville: Abingdon Press, 1941), 196.

21. Douglas Bennett, "Spirit-Anointed Preaching," *Preaching*, September—October 1989, 27.

## Chapter 4

1. Adapted from Bounds, *Preacher and Prayer*, 60-63.

2. Jonathan Edwards, *The Complete Works* (New York: Lavitt and Allen, 1855), 3:335-36.

3. Ralph G. Turnbull, *Jonathan Edwards—The Preacher* (Grand Rapids: Baker Book House, 1958), 104.

4. Spurgeon, *Lectures to My Students*, 192.

5. Ibid., 193.

6. Clarence Macartney, *Preaching Without Notes* (Nashville: Abingdon Press, 1946), 31.

7. Ibid., 23.

8. Ibid.

9. B. B. Baxter, *The Heart of the Yale Lectures* (New York: Macmillan, 1947), 219.

10. Ibid.

11. Donald G. Miller, *The Way to Biblical Preaching* (Nashville: Abingdon Press, 1957), 142.

12. Baumann, *Introduction to Contemporary Preaching*, 286.

## Chapter 5

1. Charles Colson, "My Journey from Watergate," *Christianity Today*, September 13, 1993, 96.

2. Gayle D. Erwin, *The Jesus Style*, cited in Hans Finzel, *The Top Ten Mistakes Leaders Make* (Wheaton, Ill.: Victor Books, 1994), 33.

3. Packer, "The Holy Spirit: God at Work," 30.

4. William Law, *A Serious Call to a Devout and Holy Life*, in Lechman, *Spirituality of Gentleness*, 140.

5. Stephen R. Covey, *7 Habits of Highly Effective People* (New York: Simon and Schuster, 1989), 109.

6. William Barclay, *The Gospel of John* (Philadelphia: Westminster Press, 1956), 41.

7. Oswald Chambers, *My Utmost for His Highest* (Westwood, N.J.: Barbour and Co., 1935), 58.

8. *Christianity Today*, advertisement, January 13, 1992, 49.

9. Chambers, *My Utmost for His Highest*, 58.

10. Barclay, *Gospel of John*, 47.

11. Francis Schaeffer, *No Little People* (Downers Grove, Ill.: InterVarsity Press, 1974), 68.

12. Cushman, *Hilltop Verses and Prayers*, 61.

## Chapter 6

1. Dag Hammarskjöld, "Reflections," *Christianity Today*, April 29, 1991, 31.

2. R. Paul Stevens, *Liberating the Laity* (Downers Grove, Ill.: InterVarsity Press, 1985), 38.

3. David L. McKenna, "Power to Follow, Grace to Lead," *Asbury Herald*, summer 1992, 15.

4. Wesley G. Pippert, *The Hand of the Mighty* (Grand Rapids: Baker Book House, 1991), 18.

5. Ibid., 49.

6. Peter Drucker, "Quotable Quotes," *Reader's Digest*, August 1994, 9.

7. John R. O'Neil, *The Paradox of Success* (New York: G. P. Putnam's Sons, 1993), 87.

8. John W. Gardner, *Self-Renewal* (New York: Norton and Co., 1963), 56.

9. "Quotable Quotes," *Reader's Digest*, August 1994, 29.

10. Kent Hunter, "The Quality Side of Church Growth," in *Church Growth: The State of the Art*, ed. C. Peter Wagner (Wheaton, Ill.: Tyndale House Publishers, 1986), 120.

11. Richard Foster, *Money, Sex and Power* (San Francisco: Harper and Row, 1985), 178-79.

12. Elizabeth Newby, ed., *A Philosopher's Way* (Nashville: Broadman Press, 1978), 35.

13. Jerry Mercer, "A Prayer for Servant Leaders," *Asbury Herald*, summer 1992, 6.

14. *International Thesaurus of Quotations*, ed. Rhoda Tripp (New York: Harper and Row, 1970), 774.

15. William Barclay, *The Gospel of Matthew* (Philadelphia: Westminster Press, 1958), 318.

16. William Barclay, *The Letters to the Philippians, Colossians, and Thessalonians* (Philadelphia: Westminster Press, 1959), 239.

17. McKenna, "Power to Follow, Grace to Lead," 15.

18. Mitchell, *Book of Psalms*, 7.

19. Henri Nouwen, *In the Name of Jesus* (New York: Crossroad Publishing Co., 1990), 64.

20. Ted Engstrom, *The Making of a Christian Leader* (Grand Rapids: Zondervan Publishing House, 1976), 103.

## Chapter 7

1. Bob Benson, *In Quest of the Shared Life* (Nashville: Impact Books, 1981), 76.

2. Pippert, *Hand of the Mighty,* 43.

3. Win Arn, *The Pastor's Manual for Effective Ministry* (Monrovia, Calif.: Church Growth, 1990), 8.

4. Cal Thomas, editorial, "The Church Trendy Becomes Irrelevant," *Denver Post,* March 10, 1991, Section H, 4.

5. Lechman, *Spirituality of Gentleness,* 139.

## Chapter 8

1. "Reflections," *Christianity Today,* September 16, 1991, 42.

2. Mary Strong, ed., *Letters of the Scattered Pilgrims* (San Francisco: Harper and Row, 1979), 108.

3. Marian Wright Edelman, "A Mother's Guiding Message," *Newsweek,* June 8, 1992, 40.

4. Vance Havner, *Day by Day with Vance Havner* (Grand Rapids: Baker Book House, 1953), 215.

5. "Quotable Quotes," *Reader's Digest,* September 1994, 39.

6. Bob Benson, *See You at the House* (Nashville: Generoux Nelson, 1989), 106.

7. "Looking at the World Upside Down: An Interview with Robert Coles," *Christian Century,* December 1, 1993, 1210.

8. E. Stanley Jones, *The Reconstruction of the Church—On What Pattern?* (Nashville: Abingdon Press, 1970), 95.

9. "Points to Ponder," *Reader's Digest,* March 1994, 177.

10. *Daily Bread,* February 16, 1961.

11. Jones, *Reconstruction of the Church,* 113.

## Chapter 9

1. *The Quotable Lewis,* ed. Wayne Martindale and Jerry Root (Wheaton, Ill.: Tyndale House Publishers, 1989), 431.

2. Mary Ellen Ashcroft and Holly Bridges Elliott, *Bearing Our Sorrow* (San Francisco: Harper, 1993), 121.

3. *Life in the Spirit—Mother Teresa of Calcutta,* ed. Kathryn Spink (San Francisco: Harper and Row, 1983), 57-58.

4. Warren Bennis, *Why Leaders Can't Lead* (San Francisco: Jossey-Bass, 1989), 117.

5. Frederick Buechner, *A Room Called Remember* (San Francisco: Harper and Row, 1984), 68.

6. "Points to Ponder," *Reader's Digest,* March 1991, 162.

7. *Preaching Today,* Tape No. 111, 1995.

8. "Quotable Quotes," *Reader's Digest,* May 1990, 152.

9. Robert Coles, *Harvard Diary* (New York: Crossroad, 1992), 32.

10. Robert Coles, *The Call to Service* (New York: Houghton Mifflin, 1993), 3.

11. Ibid., 30.

12. "Quotable Quotes," *Reader's Digest,* June 1991, 196.

13. Chambers, *My Utmost for His Highest,* 35.

14. Ibid., 171.

## Chapter 10

1. Barclay, *Gospel of John,* 2:149-50.

2. James F. Hind, as quoted by Josh Simon, reporter, "Who Was Jesus?" *Life* 17, No. 12 (December 1994): 79.

3. Paul S. Rees, *Don't Sleep Through the Revolution* (Waco, Tex.: Word, 1969), 58.

4. Perry Pascarella and Mark A. Frohman, *The Purpose-Driven Organization* (San Francisco: Jossey-Bass, 1989), 30.

5. Elizabeth Skoglund, *More than Coping* (Minneapolis: World Wide Publications, 1987), 6.

6. Tom Sine, *Wild Hope* (Dallas: Word Publishing, 1991), 4.